ROMANCE OF SOCIALISM AND FEMINISM

Romance of Socialism and Feminism

In Poetics of Temsula Ao, Monalisa Changkija and Robin S. Ngangom

Rosaline Jamir

SWASTIK

SWASTIK PUBLICATIONS
DELHI - 110 094 (INDIA)

ROMANCE OF SOCIALISM AND FEMINISM

First Published 2011

ISBN 978-93-80138-89-3

Published in India by

SWASTIK PUBLICATIONS
31, Gali No. 1, A-Block, Pocket-5,
CRP Water Tank, Sonia Vihar
Delhi-110094 (INDIA)
email. swastik_books@yahoo.com

Printed at: Deepak Offset Press, Delhi.

For the love of life and,
the colourful people of North-East
India....

Contents

Acknowledgements

The present treatise is a happening.

I am incredibly grateful to God, whose plans are wonderful....beyond my highest hopes.

It has taken the love, attention, and encouragement of many to have this research written, crafted and published. I was fortunate to have the assistance of many exceptional and creative minds. A few of these people include, Prof. G.D. Sharma, Pro-Vice-Chancellor, Assam University, Silchar, for scholarly inspirations; his words of encouragement still echo in my ears; Prof. N.C.R. Chandra, Head, Department of English, Nagaland University who led kindly light, on my literary journey; Dr. Tongpangkumba Ao, Director College Development Council, Nagaland University, Lumami, who pushed aside my doubts and sustained faith in me when the going was tough. Special thanks to Dr. A.J. Sebastian and Dr. N. Das, Professors, Department of English, Nagaland University, who reached out to me by way of pages and points.

Thank you! Friends, and Well-wishers for your concern and goodwill.

I remain ever indebted to Akumsashi, Imlitoshi, Office Staff of Eastern Christian College. Dimapur, and my brother Imnawapang Jamir, for their endless patience and assistance, gathering all my paper scraps and loving typing them down from the very first draft, till the finale.

My mom, Bendangla who gave me the best in life, Thank you Ma. Sangdi and Yarang, my children, who with laughter and love, were the wind beneath my wings.

—Rosaline Jamir

Preface

I have been privileged to be under the tutelage of Temsula Ao, and classmate to Monalisa and Robin. Inspired by their poetic works this book has been written with the hope that mainstream India will acknowledge the awesomeness of the poetic literature of the North-East India and learn more of the region itself, which is rich in ethos, culture and potentialities. It has also been written, with the spirit to contribute a greater awareness, of the social and feminist perspective and the need to build bridges between cultures. The edition is an Ex-po of Temsula Ao, Monalisa Changkija and Robin. S. Ngangom, three outstanding poets of the North-East India who have spent a lifetime romancing truth and beauty in their poems. The book is a literary journey and my maiden venture in the realm of writing a book, not for the sake of writing but for what lies therein? Yes, the need to know.

Temsula Ao, Monalisa Changkija and Robin S. Ngangom have designed their poetry with truth and beauty, in a simple, lucid spontaneous diction rising about all other writers of the North-Eastern Region of India. These poets have harped on the unglamorous social orders and feminine restraints that disease the region. Temsula Ao, Monalisa Changkija and R.S. Ngangom have used a gracious mode of language in their poetry, to cater to the welfare of man and society.

Now about chapter scheme of the work.

The first chapter is an introduction to North East Poetry.

A brief history of Indian English writings has been delved, thereby filtered down to the genesis of North-East writers, and thereon a review on the romance of Socialism and Feminism in the poetical works of Temsula Ao, Monalisa Changkija and Rpbin S. Ngangom.

The second chapter deals with the theory of Socialism and Feminism. Socialism as defined by Laveleye: "The aim of Socialism is man's emancipation, his restoration to the unalienated, uncrippled individual, who enters into a rich spontaneous relationship with his fellowmen and nature" is analyzed.

The context of Feminism is detailed, as 'the cry to be heard and loved' by the 'Second Sex.' If it may be said so.... if a man wanted anything said, ask a man, if a man wanted anything done, ask a woman; Feminism then, is not just words but the real action, for everything possibly good.

The third chapter is a research on the elements of Socialism and Feminism, in the poetry of Temsula Ao. The poet's gentle sensibility has been exposed in some of her poems. Her poetry is songs of verbal melody expressing sadness, pain, tragedy, ecstasy and yet the poet celebrates life. She is a thorough socialist and the most feminine of the feminists. Temsula Ao's poetry is immortal.

The fourth chapter is a enlightenment, on Monalisa Changkija's poetry. The poet's staunch devotion to crippling society and on battered and abused women, on domestic violence and women's ability to rise above the second class citizenery is researched. Monalisa Changkija is an activist, a feminist who has spoken out her beliefs without fear or favour. Her poems have been written from the heart.

The fifth chapter analyses the poetry of Robin S. Ngangom, which were mostly written in the poet's present haven, Meghalaya. The poet reminisces, nostalgically his boyhood days, his native land Manipur, and in the process questions existing social orders, the female plight, of then and now. Robin S. Ngangom is serious in his poetry and perhaps wants to indulge all readers in the seriousness.

The concluding chapter honours Temsula Ao, Monalisa Changkija and Robin S. Ngangom as excellent poets above all other writers from the North-East. They have been categorized specially, because their poetry like a gentle breeze is spiced and flavoured for a redemption, of the down-the-drain society of the present times. These poets through their poetry have drawn a silver lining behi9nd the dark clouds.

Abbreviations

a) *Tensula Ao*

1. Songs that Try to Say (1992) = STTTS
2. Songs of Many Moods (1995) = SOMM
3. Songs that Tell(1998) = STT
4. Songs from Here and There (2003) = SFHAT

b) *Monalisa Changkija*

1. Weapons of Words on Pages of Pain (1993) = WoWoPoP
2. Moonson Mourning (2007) = MM

c) *Robin S. Ngangom*

1. Time's Crossroads (1994) = TC
2. Words and the Silence (1998) = WATS
3. The Desire of Roots (2006) = TDOR

1

Introducing North-East Poetry

1. Indian Writing in English

Literature, no doubt is the manifestation of human relationships. It is circumlocutory, of what is happening in and around individuals, and in the human relationship. Poetry from time immemorial portrays human relationships as well as the relationship of man with God and nature. Poets are not mere emotional beings as many think; they are as rational as scientists. The beliefs and conventions of the society have a great bearing on the poet. The objectives of writing poetry cannot be confined to the pleasures the poet receives, by letting out his pent-up feelings. One of the professed purposes of poets everywhere and especially in India is the intellectual liberation of the Masses.

India was a legend in English, long before the English people dominated and ruled the country. We find references to India in English literature, dating back to the 16th and 17th century. The consolidation of the power of East India Company affected India in two ways. The first effect was negative because they exploited the Indian natural resources for their own profit. However the second effect was enhancing for the Indians, because of the introduction of a new concept of constitutional government, judiciary and also the English language. At the outset, the Indians reacted with apprehension towards the English language, but in time the language was given a special place in India's bosom.

The presence of English people in India promoted English literature. In 1772 Charles Grant one of the Directors of East India Company proposed the introduction of English Schools to educate the masses of illiterate Indians so that the English language would be a means of communicating western ideas. However the proposal was not supported. Nevertheless a large number of schools and colleges were opened Oriental College Ranipur (1774), Asiatic Society of Bengal Calcutta (1784), Calcutta Madrasa Calcutta (1781), to name a few.

In 1813 under the direction of the British Parliament, the East India Company assented to revive and improve literature and encourage the learned natives of India. The result was a Sanskrit School in Calcutta, which was strongly opposed by Raja Rammohun Roy. An outstanding intellectual, linguist and a social reformer, Roy in his famous *Letter on English Education* (1823), which is considered as a significant manifesto of Indian Renaissance, preferred western education in English medium to Sanskrit instruction. He was the first Indian writer who adroitly used English for castigating social evils, superstitions and rampant hypocrisy in Indian society in a clear, lucid and emphatic style. What distinguished his prose is his ability to express Indian ethos and sensibility in English. Roy is the first writer who successfully endeavoured to nativise English. According to Raja Rammohun Roy, Prince Dwarka Nath Tagore and their Brahmo Samaj companions, the English language was the sole means for a new and prosperous India.

Macaulay's famous "Minute" on Education written on 2nd Feb. 1835 *(Macaulay* ed *2005)* was a significant landmark in the history of education in India. Macaulay aimed at making natives of India good English scholars who would act as interpreters between the rulers and the ruled, a class of people, Indian in blood and colour, English in taste, opinion, moral and intellect. The "Minute", steadied the controversy between Sanskrit and English. No doubt, Sanskrit was native value. But Macaulay intended to educate Indians of the values of western literature and science. On 7th March 1835, Lord William Bentinck endorsed Macaulay's recommendations and resolved that, "the great object of the British Government ought to be the promotion of European literature and science among the natives of India and that all funds appropriated for the purpose of education would be best employed on English education alone." *(Iyengar 1990:27)*. Bentick was of the opinion that it was worth knowing English than Sanskrit or Arabic. English became the official language of India as well as the language for schools and colleges.

Sir Charles Wood was the first to realize the vital importance of the use of vernaculars in educational system. Wood's *Dispatch of 1854* emphasized that the mother tongue would be the base, but English would reign at the higher level. This *Dispatch* convened and promoted mass and female education. The result was the establishment of Universities in Bombay, Calcutta and Madras in 1857.

A middle class intelligentsia emerged from the feudal society; Indo-Anglian literature was born of the instinct of imitating English literature. The term "Indo-Anglian" was first used in 1883 when a book published in Calcutta bore the title *Indo-Anglian Literature,* containing composition from native students. *(Iyengar 1973: 3).* K.R. Srinivasa Iyengar then adopted it as the title of his debut publication on the subject *Indo-Anglian Literature* in 1943. Indo-Anglian Literature thus can be defined as literature produced in English language by Indian writers with Indian topics and locations, and thereon the Indian Renaissance.

The Indian writers in English at the outset had to face serious problems to express Indian ethos, sensibility and socio-cultural aspects in a natural, effective and convincing manner. They could spontaneously and lucidly write in their native language, because it was the language of their emotional makeup and it abundantly provided apt expression and idioms for the presentation of the multitudinous variety of Indian life. In time, the Indo-Anglian writers proved that English was not an alien language, but inevitable in Indian culture. The Indian English writers evolved the Indian style of English. Swami Vivekananda, Raja Ram Mohan Roy, Mahatma Gandhi, Jawaharlal Nehru, Shri Aurobindo, Mulk Raj Anand, R.K. Narayan, Girish Karnad, Bhabani Bhattacharya, and many other Indian English writers gave an Indian flavouring to their writings, domesticating English.

Indo-Anglian literature had to pass through many developmental stages before being recognized as a distinct genre. In the process poetry preceded fiction and drama. Poetry has always occupied a prominent place in India. The Vedic hymns chanted by the ancient sages were all beautiful poems. Poetry is written in all the existing languages including the Vernaculars. God, nature, life, death, grief, love, hope, dreams, friendship, sympathy, happiness, silence, mothers, wards, spirituality, tradition, peace, sun, water, rainbows, birth, wind, spring, nirvana, remembrance, women, sufferings, etc. Women are all frequently occurring themes in the Indian poetry. Indian poets have experienced almost all kinds of poetry including blank verse, haiku, macaronic verse, ode, lyric, villanelle, tanka and limerick.

Social concern has been of prime importance in poetry, as it has been in other parts of the world, and is one of the prominent themes in Indian poetry. Great poets of all languages through their poetry, try to awaken the suppressed. One of the most important developments in Indian poetry in the post-Independence period in all the languages has perhaps been the break-down of a single voice, a single unifying concern that despite its varieties of articulation characterized the poetry that just preceded Independence.

Some of the great Indian writers who came to be celebrated as the pioneers of modernism, later wanted to liberate them from what they thought was an overbearing literary culture. The image of the writer as the hero in the dazzling halo of the public self no more fitted the new writers who, with a different sensibility, were trying to articulate the existential tensions, anxieties, and doubts of individuals sentenced to the solitude, ambiguity and anguish of the post-industrial urban infernos.

The post-Independence era, gave a lot of exposure to the experiments in contemporary western poetry, that the Indian poets admired, yet refused to imitate, since they were well aware of the indigenous traditions that were rich in situations, characters, symbols, motifs and archetypes that could well serve, as a source of metaphors for the conflicts of modern life. Most of the Indian poets writing in English too, did not adhere to the western influence in the creative works. Constant references to tradition and redeployment of images and situations from the Epics can also be seen in the poetry of pioneers of modernism like B.S. Mardhekar and Ayyappa Panikar.

Perhaps modernism in poetry—genre with deeper roots in tradition— was not as a complete a break with the past as was modernism in fiction, a genre with a shorter history. Modernism has not crept into all genres at the same time. Unfortunately, several of our critics tend to examine modernism in general, equating the trends in all genres, thus ignoring the specific modalities of its emergence in each genre, each language and ultimately each text.

Modernism can be divided in another way too, as 'high modernism' and the avant-garde. Avant-garde is a negation of the autonomy of art as also a questioning of art itself as an institution. Avant-garde art is the art of engagement that this to reintegrate art in the practices of life. Like the modernists, the avant-garde artist also recognizes the need for technical innovation, but refuses to consider the impact of western literature, and the spread of print capitalism to have been the two major factors that contributed respectively to the shift in sensibility and the critical awareness in the characteristics of modernism. The self-conscious nature of high modernist writings is characterized by anti-mimetic and anti-organist impulses that reinforce, the aesthetic distance between the reader's habits of reading and the manner of articulation. They tend towards the lyrical and the abstract suggesting an essentialist and universalistic view of life, whereas the avant-garde idiom moves towards the discursive and the dramatic, to accommodate the multi-voiced quality of a hierarchically divided society. Literature in the Indian context is not for its own sake.

The Indian English Poetry can be divided into the following stages:

(a) The Age of Pioneers (1820-1870)

The early 19th century Indian poetry is reminiscent of the Romantics and the Victorians. Henry Louis Vivian Derozio was the earliest of the Indo-Anglian poets. His sonnets and lyrics with an Indian background were themed with topics like melancholy, death, patriotism and love. *The Faker of Jungheera (1828),* is one of Derozio's poems worth mentioning. Kashi Prasad Ghose, a contempory of Derozio was knowledgeable of English versification and his poetry, *The Shair and Other Poems (1830)* was conventional and derivative. Michael Madhusudan Dutt a more gifted poet of the era, in *Visions of the Past* in blank verse translations of *Sarmista, (1859), Ratnavali (1858),* and the farce, *Is This Called Civilization (1871),The Captive Lady (1849),* echo the poetic compositions of Wordsworth, Browning, Byron and Scott.

During the life time of Michael Madhusudan Dutt, the Dutt family had many accomplishments in literary activities. Hur Chunder Dutt published a volume of poetry called *Fugitive Pieces (1815),* which was later reprinted as *Lotus Leaves;* An anthology of 200 poems. *The Dutt Family Album (1870),* was published wherein themes were drawn from Indian history, Christian theology and Indian legends.

Contributors of this anthology were, Hur Chunder Dutt, Greece Chunder Dutt, Govin Chunder Dutt and Omesh Chunder Dutt.

(b) The Era of Indian Renaissance (1870-1900)

The poetry of this era revealed signs of development. Toru Dutt, the first great poet in Indian English poetry, revealed to "the West," the soul of India through the medium of poetry by narrating stories, sung in divine poetry thousands of years ago and created the genuine Indian atmosphere in her *Ancient Legends and Ballads of Hindustan (1882).* She has composed beautiful poems on Dhruva, Prahlad, Savitri, Sita, Laksman etc. creating the atmosphere of a bygone mythological world of the days of the *Ramayana* and the *Mahabharata.* Toru Dutt's poetry gives us the impression of the poetic potentiality within her. She was a genius in whose poetry one could find smells, sounds, sights, and ideas of the past and present nature, man lived in. According to Iyengar, "Toru has left behind her, an achievement to which it will be difficult to find a parallel in the history of English literature." (*1946:17)*

Swami Ramatirtha and Swami Vivekananda have also composed a number of powerful, spiritual and mystical lyrics in English. Some of Swami Vivekananda's poems are, *Quest for God (1893), My Play is Done (1895), Angels Unawares (1898), To the Awakened India (1898), Requiescat in Pace (1898).* The last poem was written in memoriam to J.J. Goodwin. The Swami is regarded as one of India's foremost nation builders. His teachings and writings influenced the building of national leaders and philosophers, a few of who were Mahatma Gandhi, Jawaharlal Nehru, Subhas Chandra Bose, Aurobindo and Radhakrishnan. Vivekananda's poetry was a blend, of a rational mind with religious temperament.

(c) The Era of Political Awakening (1900-1947)

Poets of this era have themed their poems on patriotism

and political awakening, inspired by the freedom movement of India. Manmohan Ghose, Rabindranath Tagore, Sri Aurobindo, Sarojini Naidu and H. N. Chattopadhyaya were the distinguished poets of this period. Manmohan Ghose wrote various poems on various themes, but the themes of love of nature and the love of man which are interwoven, reigns supreme in his poems. The English language was mother tongue for him. His collection of poetry are namely *Primavera (1890), Love Songs and Elegies (1898), and Songs of Life and Death,* which was published posthumously in 1926.

Rabindranath Tagore, who is without question the greatest songwriter and lyrical genius of modern India, was the one who first gained for India a place on the world literary scene through some of his finest creations like *The Gardener (1913), Gitanjali (1913), The Crescent Moon(1913), Fruit Gathering (1916), Lover's Gift (1918)* and *Crossing (1918).* His poetry is mainly lyrical; his lyrics are simple, sublime, serious and majestic representing the quintessence of India's hoary past.

Sri Aurobindo, the great seer of Pondicherry, made abiding contribution to Indian English poetry by virtue of his narrative power, polished and refined diction, and bold metrical experiments. Sri Aurobindo's poetic output was varied. He wrote lyrics, narrative and philosophical poems and poetic plays. *Savitri (1947)*, his Magnum Opus, is the greatest epic in Indian English poetry. The epic was originally to be a simple narrative poem of two parts: the first part, with Earth, for its scene of action and the second part carrying the action into the world of Night, Twilight and Day. But the poem came out as long narrative poem making it one of the largest epics of the world. Iyengar rightly comments "Considered merely as a poet and critic of poetry, Sri Aurobindo would still rank among the supreme masters of our time." *(1990:153)*

Sarojini Naidu, 'Bul Bul Hind' or the 'Nightingale of India' has presented the rich and colorful panorama of

Indian culture in her poems. She vividly recreates the romance of Indian weavers, the gay Coromandel fishermen, the snake charmer, the Indian dancers, the India of temples, wandering pilgrims and singers, the sights and sounds familiar around man, the purdah nashin, the bangle sellers, the palanquin bearers, the village folks, Raksha bandhan, Vasantpanchmi, Divali and Nagpanchmi. Naidu's *The Golden Threshold (1905), The Bird of Time (1912)* and *The Broken Wing (1917)* and *Feast of Youth (1918)*, are some of her finest versifications. Various facets of Islam and Muslim life are fairly dealt with in, *Prayer of Islam (1915)*. Indian mysticism is echoed in, *In Salutation to Eternal Peace (1917), The Soul's Prayer (1917)* and *To a Buddha Seated on a Lotus (1917)*. Sarojini Naidu's poems show the influence of the Romantic English poets in essence, despite her presentation of an Indian atmosphere.

Harindranath Chattopadhyaya's collection of poems are: *The Feast of Youth (1918), The Magic Tree (1920), Grey Clouds and White Showers (1922-24), Poems and Plays (1927), Strange Journey (1936), The Dark Well (1939), Edgeways and the Saint (1946), A Treasury of Poems (1948), Spring in Winter (1956), Masks and Farewells (1961)* and *Virgins and Vineyards (1967)*. His poetry is remarkable for thematic variety, and also the combination of Aurobindonian and Marxian mysticism. The Indian soul is found in the rhythms of the English tongue in the poetry of Chattopadhyaya. During this era there were many philosophers who turned to writing poetry, thereby going for a change.

Brajendranath Seal, a philosopher wrote the poem *The Quest Eternal (1939)* which combined reason and imagination. Surendranath Dasgupta, another philosopher also wrote poems. His poem *The Vanishing Lines (1956)* gives us a panoramic view of the soul's landscape. K.M. Panikkar's *The Waves of Thought (1944)* is a ruminative poem. Under the sway of Sri Aurobindo, others who wrote poetry were, Nirodbaran *Sun-Blossoms (1947)*, K.D. Sethna *Artist Love*

(1925), The Secret Splendor (1940) and The Adventure of the Apocalypse (1949), Anilbaran Roy *Song from the Soul (1939),* Nolini Kanta Gupta *To the Heights (1944)* Dilip Kumar Roy *Eyes of Light (1948), The Immortals of Bhagavat (1958),* Amrita *Visions and Voices (1929).*

Poets of this age wrote on patriotism, romance, Indian legends and philosophy. The poems communicate the picturesque, sensuous and beauty of landscapes and variegated aspects of India. These Indian poets have evolved a distinct idiom to express their poetic sensibility. Though their poetry was infused with an Indianness yet these poets were Romantics, divorcing contemporary problems and reality in substance. Poetry of the pre-independence period was a mass of sentiments, clichés, outdated language and conventions, the ossified remains of a colonial tradition badly in need of a new start through grafting on a vital body of contemporary verse and contact with contemporary life and speech.

(d) The Era of Independence or The Modern Poetry (1947-)

Modern Indian English-language poetry is one of the many new literatures, which began to emerge at the end of the Second World War after the end of colonialism. Indian poetry of this period is remarkable for fecundity, experimentation and the vivid presentation of contemporary reality and consciousness which was the result of the traumatic political situation arising out of the partition of the country, rapid urbanization and industrialization, disintegration of village community, change in cultural and social values. Contemporary Indian poetry of this era was also influenced by western thoughts – Existentialism, Positivism, Phenomenology, Surrealism and the New Aesthetics, which lifted Indian poets from an exclusive to an extensive range of creative experience; conservative to a cosmopolitan culture and to confront the new shape of things and acquire a new view of human destiny. The times that are a changing required a new image and this was largely been focused upon by the modern poets.

If at first, modern Indian English poetry appeared to be indebted to British and a few European models, it now revealed an awareness of most of world literature, including contemporary American, and recent South American. The influence of the Romantics and Victorians were replaced by Walt Whitman, T.S. Eliot, Ezra Pound and Y.B. Yeats. The new poetry was attuned to the temper of the new age, nothing compared to the colours, smells and honeyed light, of the poetry of the era of Political Awakening. Freshness, sensibility, trained intelligence and vitality were the characteristics of the modern poetry. Poets who wrote brilliantly, Indo-Anglian poetry were, Nissim Ezekiel, K.Raghavendra Rao, Dom Moraes, A.K. Ramanujan, V.D. Trivedi, Leela Dharmraj, P. Lal, Kamala Das, Adil Jussawalla, Vikram Seth, Jayant Mahapatra, G.S. Sharat Chandra, R. Parathasarathy, Shiv K. Kumar, Keki N. Daruwalla, Arvind Krishna Mehrotra, Gieve Patel, Arun Kolatkar, Dilip Chitre, Pritish Nandy, O.P. Bhatanagar, Margaret Chatterjee, Santan Rodrigues, Manohar Shetty, Vikram Seth and Saleem Peeradina.

Nissim Ezekiel is one of the most towering figures in modern Indian English poetry, giving it a new dimension by extending its scope and range. His poems are an expression of the intellectual and ethical note, penning the experience of educated urban Indians, discarding provincial, mythological and chauvinistic sentiments. Ezekiel's poetry collection consists of *A Time to Change (1952), Sixty Poems (1953), The Third (1959), The Unfinished Man (1960), The Exact Name (1965), Hymns in Darkness (1976), Latter-day Psalms (1982),* and *Collected Poems (1989).* As a poet, Ezekiel exalted the American poetic tradition, tracing back to Whitman, and advocated cultural synthesis. Ezekiel made poetry the pivot point of his life and in all his poems he leaves the impression of an urban poet, the poet of the great metropolis- Bombay, the place where he has been living since his birth.

Dominic Francis Moraes, popularly known as Dom Moraes, was renowned for his imagination which coloured his poetry. His works include, *Poems (1960)*, *John Nobody (1965)*, *Beldam & Others (1967)*, *Absences (1983)*, *Collected Poems (1987)*, *Serendip (1990)*, *Out of God's Oven: Travels in a Fractured Land (1992)*, *The Long Strider (2003)*, *Never at Home, memoir, My Son's Father, memoir, A Variety of Absences: The Collected Memoirs of Dom Moraes (2003)*, *Typed With One Finger (2003)*, *Collected Poems:* 1954-2004 *(2004)*,

A.K. Ramanujan, combined tradition and modernity in his poetry. His poems *The Striders (1966)* and *Relations (1971)*, is coloured with the Indian experience and sensibility with touches of family, local places and beliefs, yet having the modern stance of skepticism and irony. Ramanujan's poems have a highly accomplished, understated preciseness and economy of statement, symbol and narrative. Without an obvious formality of structure his poems seemed perfectly formed showing a range of technique beyond that of any previous Indian English poetry. Ramanujan is a traditionalist, and his poetry has been influenced by his Hindu heritage. Family images painted his poetry and in this respect he is comparable to Ezekiel, both the poets being committed to the Indian reality.

In poetry the phrase "Poets' poet", mean poets who have been inspired by other poets. P. Lal is of this category, with the purpose of encouraging creative writing in English and trans-creation in India. Lal called, for the poetry of the spirit, the poetry of the earth, both sacred and secular poetry both the epics of the soul and the lyrics of everyday life. He has contributed much in the field of poetry, some of which are *The Parrot's Death and Other Poems (1960 & 1998)*, *Love's the First (1962* and *1998)*, *Change! They Said (1966* and *1998)*, *Draupadi and Jayadratha and*

Others Poems (1967 and *1998), Yakshi from Didarganj and Others Poems (1969), The Man of Dharma and the Rasa of Silence (1974* and *1998), The Collected Poems of P.Lal (1977* and *1998),* and *Calcutta: a long poem (1978* and *1998).* Besides these volumes of poetry, Lal was editor to, *Indian Poetry in English: An Anthology (1969)* containing the poems of over 130 poets.

Kamala Das is the pioneer poet who gave a precise and candid expression to feminine sensibility in all its variety. Though her poetic works consist only three volumes viz. *Summer in Calcutta (1965), The Descendants (1967)* and *The Old Playhouse and other poems (1973),* Kamala Das has become the mouthpiece of feminist struggle against traditional values imposed on women, demanding social justice, sexual equality and equal rights for the second sex. She looks at man and woman as individuals and that women need freedom for themselves from the patriarchal history. Her poetry is autobiographical and confessional, which exposes a world that is sterile, arid, dehumanized because of the sheer absence of love. Kamala Das had her own version of the contemporary confessional mode, practiced by such American poets as Robert Lowell and Sylvia Plath.

Keki N. Daruwalla is one of the most substantial Indian English poets. He celebrated the writing of poetry as personal, exploring one's interior world and yet having a social gesture. A police officer by profession, he portrays transparently the contemporary Indian socio-political world, ravaged with riots, exploitation, greed, crimes and corruption in free India. His poetical works include *Under Orian (1976), Affaritian in April (1971), Crossing of Rivers (1976), Winter Poems (1980), The Keeper of the Road (1982) and Landscapes (1987).* Vikram Seth's poetry has been regarded as a overseas collection of Indian Literature evolved in its own way. He has rapidly risen into prominence with *Mappings(1982),The Humble Administrators Garden (1985),* a and *The Golden Gate (1986),* the latter a witty novel in verse.

Among the poets of the avant-grade were A.K. Mehrotra, Arun Kolatkar, Dilip Chitre, Mahapatra, Pritiosh Nandy and Deba Patnaik. Arvind Krishna Mehrotra, was well read and so his contributions to English Indian poetry were great. Believing that, poetry is perception's flames, his works include *BharatMata: A Prayer (1966)*, *Woodcuts on Paper (1967)*, *Pomes | Poems | Poemas (1971)*, *Three (1973)*, *The Absent Traveller: Prakrit Love Poetry from the Gathasaptasati of Satavahana Hala (1991)*. Jayant Mahapatra's poetry is an eloquent expression of the eternal silence of the Unknown. He is an original, prolific poet, remarkable for depth of feelings, and true poetic imagination. *Swayamvara and other Poems (1971), A Rain of Rites (1974), Waiting (1979), The False Start (1980), Life Signs (1983)* are some of Mahapatra's poetic volumes. His poems are an expression of his inner world and problems, about the relationship between the self and reality. *Relationship (1981)* was his masterpiece and is indeed, a modern epic.

O.P. Bhatanagar is a common man's poet. His poems highlight contemporary social reality and human predicaments. They are charged with agony, agitation and aggression, because Bhatanagar had a humanitarian object and illusions a better tomorrow for mankind with a more humane community. His volumes of poems are namely *Feeling Fossils (1977), Angels of Retreats (1980), Oneiric Vision (1980), Shadows in Floodlights (1984), The Audible Landscape (1986)* and the most recent-*Cooling Flames of Darkness (2001)*. Bhatanagar has been a part of an avante-grade. He was the kind of poet who felt that, every poet needed to sharpen his style to speak out the truth of human character and life. C.P.Surendran, a very much poet of today, is the author of three volumes of poetry which are *Gemini II (1994)*, *Posthomos Poems (1999), Canaries on the Moon (2002)*.

Besides these stalwarts, I.H. Rizvi, M.N. Sharma, Suresh Kholi, Deb Kumar Das, Ruskin Bond, K. Raghvendra Rao, R. K. Singh, Syed Ameenuddin, Krishna Srinivas and many others have also contributed to the prospects of poetry.

The modern Indian Poetry is heterogeneous in nature. Some of the catalytic forces permeating the modern Indian poetry are the variety of movements and counter movements, the variety of Indian sources, foreign influences surrounding it and its varied social world that shapes the lives of the poets. The modern age poets do not give any political or social message, nor plunge onto realms of aesthetics, but they firmly grapple with contemporary political and social tensions. The era of independence, has given birth to the kind of poetry that is remarkable for fecundity, experimentation and the vivid presentation of contemporary reality and consciousness.

The poets of today's India have risen from a conservative to a cosmopolitan culture, to confront the new shape of things and acquire a new view of human image and destiny. The value of human personality, which the social, economic and political trends of the 20th century threaten to submerge have been revived. These poets have brought a new awareness to English poetry. It is poetry of protest significant in subject matter and expression. The wreckage of human civilization, the infidelity of man, and the resultant catastrophe are the recurrent themes. Poetry was written on concrete terms and experience that was intellectual as well emotional, in precise, lucid and tangible expression. The language was the current pattern of speech. The Indian writers have used native expression and words in English structures in order to nativize English. This is termed as the used of *loan words* from Hindi and other Indian languages so that the aspects of Indian life, society and sensibility could be done in exact expression. This mode of English expression cultivated a new idiom, style and mode of expression in commensurate with the genius of India. It enabled them to present a veracious and veritable picture of India and her people before the West. Indian

Poetry was free from propaganda, imitation and rationally written.

The profession of poetry is a consecrated endeavor and an exacting discipline. It was to the credit of the new poets, that they were prepared to take their vocation seriously. Each poet revealed a quest for an identity, they are all individual poets and yet, all having a common identity; the Indianess. At the present times, Indian English poetry is a part of the process of modernization which includes urbanization, industrialization, mobility, independence, social change, increased communication (in the form of films, televisions, radio, journals and newspapers), national and international transportation networks, mass education and participation in issues of the international modern world. English is no longer the language of colonial rulers; it is a language of modern India in which words and expressions have recognized national rather than imported significances and references, alluding to local realities, traditions and ways of feeling. Today, the most outstanding achievement of Indian English poets is the creative adaption of English, to Indian needs and the assertion of an Indian identity by dealing with Indian, issues in their very own inimitable style, thus leaving an imperishable mark in modern poetry and opening a bright, glorious and immense future for the new Indian English poetry.

2. Poetry of the North-East India: An Overview

The North-East Region of India comprising eight states *viz.* Arunachal Pradesh, Assam, Manipur, Meghalaya, Mizoram, Nagaland, Sikkim, and Tripura is geographically isolated, linked to the last of the country by the narrow Siliguri corridor. North-East India has long been known for its uniqueness, the homeland of diverse tribes and communities and cultures and languages and yet up to a point has a shared history. The North-Eastern part of India has no specific history of writings in English. In the absence of a common language the influence of Christian missionaries in the 19th century introducing English, became the vital means of communication for all the states. Anyone venturing into the sea of North-East Indian poetry would notice that English has occupied the foremost place among the different languages in which poetry is written.

In the histories of Indian English literature written, by K.R.S. Iyengar and M.K. Naik, there is no mention of North-East literary inputs. There is just only a mention of Praphulladatta Goswami's *Bihu Songs of Assam (1957).* From the North-East Region, the first attempt to collect and translate the folk songs of the region was by an Assam folklorist, Praphulladatta Goswami in 1957, when he published his *Bihu Songs of Assam.* In 1960 Hem Barua published his *Modern Assamese Poetry* which included the English translations from twenty six Assamese poets of which nine of these poets rendered their own poems in English. Some commendable works were *Songs and Tales of North East India* (ed) by P. Goswami (published by the Folklore Society of Assam, Guwahati, *1976*) and *Folk Music and Folklore-An Anthology (ed)* Hemanga Biswas (Folk Music and Folklore Research Institute, Calcutta, *1967*). Since the 1950's Late Hem Baruah., Late Navakanta Baruah, Ajit Baruah and some others have translated some Assamese poetry into English. Other commendable works that were translated by Pradip Acharya were poems of Hiren Battacharya named *Ancient Gongs* (Beaver Books Publication, Guwahati, *1985*), and Dr. Bhupen Hazarika's selected poems- *Where Seas Meet* (Lawyers' Book Stall, Guwahati, *1993*). He has also enlightened the translation of 33 Assamese poets from Navakanta Barua (b.1926) to Hemanga Dutta (b. 1973) in the Sahitya Akademi's *Indian Literature (*Vol. 177. Jan– Feb 1997) under the title *The Renaissance of Elegy:*Assamese poetry from 1975 to 1999 in the *Indian Literature, Vol-179 (May-June 1997).* Manipuri and Khasi peotry respectively were translated by Robin S. Ngangom and Desmond.L.Kharmawphalang. Robin S. Ngangom has translated selected poems of 20 Manipuri poets. Desmond.L.Kharmawphalang published a bilingual (Khasi-English) edition of his poems entitled *Touchstone* in 1986. Furthermore selected folk songs from Mizo, Ao-Naga, Zo, Khasi, Tarlong, Abatani and Nokte had been translated into English by C.S. Row Riengsete and Abhik Gupta, Temsula Ao, M.G. Munluo and, Vincent Darlong respectively. The poetry of Tripura in English translation has been presented by Sisir Sinha in *Indian Literature Vol-I 191.*

The writings in English by writers from the North-East part of India have been neglected by critics because of their meager production. But as of today, the multi- ethnic poets of the North-East Region have found a name in Indian English Literature, (Revised M.A.(English) syllabus of Delhi University 2003 the Poetry of Desmond L. Kharmawphang, and in the same of IGNOU, Shillong, the poetry by the writers of Nagaland have been incorporated).

More than two dozen of poets from various provinces of the North-Eastern part of India, have published their poems and poetry collections in English, both in India and abroad. These poets have been called "ethnic poets" *(Guha 2000:p.119)*. Nigamananda Das "call them multi-ethnic poets because they hail from multi-various ethnic groups and their chief concern is ethnicity. Hills, valleys, men, myths, legends, communal violence, tribal rites, mystic and profoundly aesthetic sensibilities, ecology, self-alienation, autobiographical exegesis of self being some of the themes of their poetry, the poets are consistently home-bound pilgrims." *(Das 2004 :p.1)*

The multi-ethnic poets of the region since 1980 have been exposing the ethos of their land and communities in their poetry. Mrs. Lakshahira Das, Dayananda Pathak, Late Umakanta Sarma, Bhupati Das (from Assam), Anjum Hasan, Desmond L. Kharmawphlang, Kynpham Singh Nongkynrih, Ananya S. Guha (from Meghalaya), Temsula Ao, Nini Vingurian Lungalang, Monalisa Changkija and Easterine Iralu (from Nagaland), Mamang Dai, Yumlam

Tana (from Arunachal Pradesh), Robin S. Ngangom, R. K. Madhubir (from Manipur), H. Ramdinthari, Mona Zote (from Mizoram), Rajendra Bhandari (from Sikkim) and Bhaskar Roy Barman (from Tripura) are the representative poets who have been contributing to the multi-ethnic North-Eastern Indian English poetry.

Lakshahira Das, Dayananda Pathak, Late Umakanta Sarma, Bhupati Das, the poets from Assam have exposed the mysteries surrounding life and tradition. Two other elder poets are late Maheswar Neog (1918-1995) and Amaresh Datta (1920 -). Late Maheswar Neog's collection of English poetry titled *Under One Sky (1970)* is an occasional celebration of poetic passions. Amaresh Datta is an internationally famed personality, who has been honoured by the International Association of Poetry of Rome for his poetry. He is the Ex-Chief Editor of *Encyclopedia of Indian Literatures,* Sahitya Akademi. He has to his credit a collection of English poetry titled *Captive Moments (1971)* and two verse dramas. Lakshahira Das, a renowned poet and singer of Assam has published one collection of poetry in English entitled *Between Birds (1990)*. Bhupati Das, a fine lyricist and a mystic poet has published two collections of poetry in English entitled *May I (1998)* and *Life and Beyond (2004)*. Dayananda Pathak, a poet, orator and critic all in one has published a volume of English poetry *Coral Island (1998)*. The second volume of his poetry titled *The Golden Deer* is yet to be published. Late Umakanta Sarma has to his credit a single collection of poetry in English entitled *Throwing out (1998)*.

The poets of Meghalaya, namely, Anjum Hasan, Desmond L. Kharmawphlang, Kynpham Sing Nongkynrih, Ananya S. Guha, Esther Syiem, Paul Lyngdoh, Indari Syiem Warjri are some of the poets who have delved on the legends, events and ecology of their land. Kynpham Sing Nongkynrih has written two volumes of poetry-*Moments (1992)* and *The Sieve (1992)* wherein he mirrors the cultural and ecological heritage of Meghalaya. Desmond L.

Kharmawphlang has published three collection of poetry in English namely *Touchstone (1987), Here (1992)* and *Coming Home (1996)*. His poems relate concerns about contemporary social culture and environmental imbalance. Ananya S. Guha has three collections of poetry titled *In This My Land (1986), What Else is Alive? (1998) Poems (1997)*. Anjum Hasan, Esther Syiem, Syiem Warjri are all poets of their nativeland.

Temsula Ao, Nini Vingurian Lungalang, Easterine Iralu, Monalisa Changkija, the poets of Nagaland have painted their poetry with the glories, mysteries, legends and landscapes of their land. Temsula Ao celebrates nature, moments, love and sadness in her poetry. Her collections of poetry are, *Songs That Tell (1988), Songs That Try to Say (1992), Songs of Many Moods (1995)* and *Songs from Here and There (2003)*. Nini Vingurian Lungalang has a collection of poetry entitled *The Morning Years (1994)* which is an impression of tribal life, the neglected people and the Naga heritage. Easterine Iralu has published two poetry collections entitled *Kelhoukevira (1982)* and *The Windhover Collection (2001)*. Monalisa Changkija has two publications of poetry, namely *Weapons of Words on Pages of pain (1993)* and *Monsoon Mourning (2007)*. Her poetry is an eye opening view of a society and everything within.

Mamang Dai and Yumlam Tana from Arunachal Pradesh with faith have stretched out in the dark for an identity, in their poetry. Dai's collection of poetry, *River Poems (2004)* enlightens life in Arunachal Pradesh, the geography of the state, the glorious past and the present living. She is a thorough nature-loving humanist, who finds a profound serenity in nature besides being a keen explorer of heritage, sentimental of traditional tribal values. Yumlam Tana has a collection of poetry entitled *The Man and The Tiger (2000)* which is an expression of Arunachal's tribal culture. In his poetry there is a constant clinging to the mores of quest for identity, a major concern of post-colonial Indian English literature.

Robin S. Ngangom and R. K. Madhubir are poets from Manipur narrating the gravity of events of the North-East. North-East comes alive in the poetry of Robin S. Ngangom. He has to his credit three collections of poems namely *Time's Crossroads (1994), Words and The Silence (1998)* and *The Desire of Roots (2006).* R. K. Madhubir has published three collections of poetry in English entitled *The H-hour Patient and Other Poems (1982), The Time Bomb and Other Poems (1987)* and *The Shadow of Darkness (1998).* Madhubir in his poetry is apprehensive, with the five W's i.e. women, wealth, wine, war and world.

The poetry of H. Ramdinthari, Mona Zote from Mizoram is basically of nature and environmental-friendly themes. Both have yet to publish their first collection of poetry. The landscape of Mizoram haunts the vision of both the poets constantly. In the quest of poetic realities, they have invested novel images drawn from the ecology and culture of the land. Poets from Sikkim and Tripura have also been homebound in their versification. Rajendra Bhandari the lone poet from Sikkim has a wide publication of his English poetry. The scenic beauty of Sikkim, the mountain clouds, snow and the rains, arresting the attention of people from different parts of the world have become a continual source of inspiration for the artistic creativity to Bhandari. The tribal ethos of Tripura, are best exposed in the poetry of Bhaskar Roy Barman. Recurrence of river, stream, mountain, tree, temple, priest, crow, stone and other forms of ecology is found in many of his poems. Through these images, the poet symbolically exposes the hard life of the tribes and their happy singing life in the midst of all hardships. His first collection of poetry entitled *Fragrance* is under publication from London.

Like other new literatures, the literature of the North-East is a newly emerging literature of India. The North-East Poetry is one whole and not the poetry of Nagaland or the poetry of Meghalaya alone; it is because of the fact that the English language enables the making of poets in the entire North East region and thus the emergence of North-East poetry. The literature of this region, contribute to the national literature of India which in turn promotes the multi-ethnic, multi-racial, multi-cultural fabric of Indian literature. The writers from the North-East Region differ from his counterpart in the mainland in a significant way. North-East poetry springs from cruel contradictions of the land, folk traditions, The Hill world, all hemmed in by extreme realism.

At the most, the poetry of North-East mirror the body and mind of the times, remedying none to get on in life, but inspiring and moving, so that anyone can perhaps undergo a change after having read a meaningful poem. The mainland poet analyzes tradition, culture, philosophy, and perhaps a little of wickedness around. North-East poet lives with the threat of corruption, and terror, which ultimately paints his poetry. North-Eastern India is in great ferment today. A society that is under moral and social degradation, with the quest for truth and liberty, is exposed. Besides, the social unrest that has become endemic of this region has manifold areas of similarity. The common man is in agony, while the rich are afraid and the middle class are striving. Though many writers have come up from these similar sorts of experiences, their literary works are unique to themselves. North-East poetry has been definitely shaped by the social upheavals that its people, are living through and yet, each poet has his or her own perspective and distinctive point of view. Furthermore, the compromising factor of the North-East poets is that most have romanced with Socialism and Feminism in their literary works.

Perhaps the characteristic most central to the definition of North-East poetry is its unwillingness to be defined, labeled, or nailed down. On reading poetry by the North-East poet, who experiences 'the spontaneous overflow of powerful feelings' the reader might disagree with most of the traditional definitions of poetry. The North-East poet does not make the reader's body cold; instead it sets fire to the reader's mind and soul. The unwillingness of the poets to succumb to the social inequality, injustice, exploitation, and slavery are in turn transmitted into the hearts of the readers. While it may not make him a better writer, living with the menace of the gun, he cannot merely indulge in verbal wizardly and woolly aesthetics yet he must perforce master the art of witness. As a natural aftermath to the above, our society has been reduced to a mute witness to the banality of corruption and terror. The poets cannot be expected to promote ethnic harmony as a part of his writing programme. Yet, the focal point of literature of the North-East is as *Czeslaw Milosz* asked:

What is poetry, which does not save

Nations or people? (www.poetryfoundation.org/archive/poem.html?id=179569)

And yet, even though literature cannot bring about harmony or a moral change, the double challenge of truth and liberty, propounded by Socialism is dared. Socialism is the flow of human goodwill to keep social life free from friction. Most North-East poets have themed their poems on Socialism which is the quest for truth, liberty, social progress and a remedy for the existing disorders. Furthermore, Feminism has been tiptoed on. Woman, the Second Sex, was pedestal by the feminist movement in 1872 by way of a pamphlet: '*L Homme Femme*' by Alexander Dumas, the younger. For centuries the position and role of women has been distorted. Today, the equal challenge has been taken up by the North-East writers, thus recognizing the value and assets of the Second Sex.

The ethnic, linguistic, literary and cultural diversity of the North-East part of India are rebounding themes in the poetry of most of the North-East poets and especially that of Temsula Ao, Robin S. Ngangom and Monalisa Changkija. Though meager in quantity, the poetry of Temsula Ao,

Monalisa Changkija, and Robin S. Ngangom voices the major values of the modern living conditions of the North-East. These gems were lying at the bottom of the sea unnoticed till the North-East poetry came into limelight with the publication of a journal entitled *New Frontiers* by the North-East Writers Forum on 15th August 1998. Temsula Ao, Monalisa Changkija, and Robin S. Ngangom are poets, with definite purposes in their lives.

The 'socio-cultural devastations' deep rooted in the daily existence of the modern man where the intricacies of life never take departures into the background of the 'minimum' rather moving with temperamental tensions into the zenith of 'complex coincidences', never get itself remedied through the moral edifice on which each society is expected to be built. The anguish and anger of an era, largely tortured by the norms and dictates of the very specific socio-political situations prevalent there, get itself voiced through the poems of Temsula Ao, where, apart from the social deformities, even the physical and psychological invasions and insurgence which have become part of the feminine experience from days not dated, get portrayed and in its turn it becomes 'the scream' germinating not out of the physical torture, rather the psychological and emotional outburst. Temsula Ao's poetry, on the one hand a mode of resistance to the 'unacceptable' in the social as well as personal life of the individual, on the other hand becomes a mode of representation of the hitherto 'unacknowledged' and often neglected and sidelined aspects of life. The reformation that forms part of the expectation of the masses for the better social living which is not evaluated merely on the basis of the material progress, rather as a functional process through which the synthesis of the personal life and the social life can be attained in the form of a harmonious existence where the term tranquility or equilibrium is of higher significance, by denoting the ever cherished dream of the people that has been remaining as an 'absence' in their life. Temsula Ao's poetry, through the eradication of certain conventions and codes of conduct prescribed by the male dominated society, especially for the purpose of a female suppression, never envisions a paradise for the female in the near future, rather never losing hope of the advent of better days for the female, she lays down the requirements and prerequisites that are essential for the establishment of a world where the female will be 'more free' to the extent of asserting her individuality and identity, the absence of which made her 'impotent' in the 'barren' social life. Through the emancipation of the female she expects an 'evaporation' of the false prejudices and petty hypocrisies that an individual possess for another and in its larger dimensions expressing itself as the symptoms of social degeneration and degradation.

Temsula Ao's poetry opens up a window, on the world of a feminine psyche where the consciousness of the female, which is suppressed mainly through the commercial instincts of the modern generation experiences a kind of deterioration which is a kind of progression to a large degradation, through the loss of chance for an emotional response leading to a kind of decline from feeling to the bare rationalism. Temsula Ao is of the opinion that the majority of a female's recollections are associated with the existence and then the loss of some important element of freedom of an identity, of a stable existence of their day today existence and each of the changes, whether it is in the social, economic, cultural or political sphere evokes in her a sense of loss especially of security and order resulting in a 'silent protest'. As Louis Rubin presents the contrasts of a geographical region called, America in his essay, *A Tragedy of Two Lost Women (Rubin 1982:188-89),* Temsula Ao through her poetry portrays the language, landscape, culture and complexities of the Indian landscape, through which she draws the attention of the readers to the larger social issues especially to the feminine cause. Thus her poetry is an ample expression of the female in the social context and voices the concept of Socialism.

The socio-cultural transformations, which may equip one with better force for a social competence or can have an adverse effect on who is not the fittest in the society, undoubtedly establishes some sort of reverberations in one's life, through which either the well being or the devastation of the individual or the society is ensured. The moulding nature of the modern era, in accordance with its concepts regarding what or how an individual should be, becomes highly instrumental in the exasperations and exhaustions experienced by a generation as the process of moulding exerts excessive pressure to initiate flexibility in the newly ordained mould. The automatized existence of the people of the present social scenario is brought under the transparency of the public scrutiny in the poetry of Monalisa Changkija where, according to her, the social barrier and even the geographically set boundaries diminish in the collective effort of the female suppression through which the socialist order is brought under the deterioration. Monalisa Chankija's poetry provides one with a cross section of the sabotage happening in the society and thus flogs the hypocritical tendencies inherent in the social behaviour and which like a melanoma leads to a cancerous decay in the society affecting mainly the weak and the poor and thus having its severe traumatic effect on the female.

Just as Maxwell Geismare, speaks of the emergence of the modern industrial order and the decay of the southern landed aristocracy in America in his work *Writers in Crisis (Geismare 1942),* Monalisa Changkija, through her poetry speaks of the adverse effects of the modern industrial culture on the present generation, affecting their lives to a degree which is far from being positively influential. The tone of the poet, while speaking of the never to be appreciated tendencies of the society may not be a mellifluous one, but even there is no calculated scheme of pricking any one rather the frustration of the poet finds an outlet in the poetic mode and which, according to her may assist the general public in their dreams of a day where everything will be governed largely by the socialist temperament and which will ensure the eradication of the megalomaniac tendencies to ensure the equal pedestal to everyone in the social life.

Monalisa Changkija never deviates into the metaphysical or the extraterrestrial while dealing with the thematic concerns in her poetry, but while understanding a musing on the poetry of Monalisa Changkija, one may be flabbergasted to find the inbuilt treasure of the themes, which, defying all the attempts of confinement evolves out of nothing to a greatness as we find of the paintings of Salvador Dali detailed in *Spirit and Matter* by Pro. Joseph. S. Rendulich *(Rendulich 2004),* where apart from the surface level simplicity of the paintings one may come to encounter the metaphysical dimensions of it, by which the real beauty and depth of the artistry is revealed.

Monalisa Changkija's poetry has got multitudinous dimensions and tendencies as, on the one hand it becomes a revelation of the 'female' in her totality and on the other hand it is a heartfelt cry for a progressive Socialism in every sphere of life. Amidst the duplication of the modern life, Monalisa Changkija's poetry becomes a different voice with its celebration of Socialism and to denunciation of any kind of autocratic tendencies, which according to her may spell the doom of the society. Thus, Monalisa Changkija's poetry through a revelation ensures a realization of the female and Socialism.

The poetic world of any poet is the result of a series conflicts originating out of the antithetical forces, that pull the poetic mind in different dimensions often disturbing it to the extent of making the poet unable to decide, upon what is right and wrong and thus the poet sheds the emotional turbulences into the language of poetry resulting in the creation of a piece of poetry The contextual or situational forces make a tremendous impact in the germination of any good piece of art, as they become the visible embodiment of the very concrete experience, the absence of which may characterize the work of art with certain "absences" especially the absence of 'life' or originality.

In this respect the poetry of Robin S. Ngangom bears the mark of a full-fledged life and energy as his poetry is not the result of mere figment, rather the offspring of the very stark realities and concrete experiences that are gathered mostly from the geographical region which has witnesses perpetual conflicts, agitations and the resultant agonies of which he too is a participant. The incongruence nature of the socio-political atmosphere of the worth with its claims of diversity and metaphoric implications find an apt representation in the poetry of Robin S. Ngangom and he, like many other writers of the era finds the sediment of these conflicts with all its sediment and gravity in the person of the female, where she becomes deprived of what is to be the agent to safeguard the society through the protection of its microcosm the family especially by taking upon herself what actually does not belong to her, but which has to be borne for the larger interests of the society. As Leela Dubey speaks of the adverse effect of caste system, which in its turns affecting mainly the female, in her celebrated essay, *Caste and Woman (Dubey 1996),* Robin S. Ngangom too, finds the scurrilous attacks on the female devastating all the possibilities of a socialist order of society.

The poetry of Robin S. Ngangom may be considered, as a dissection of the social fabric which diagnoses the degeneracy of it, for the apt supply of the remedy and he finds that the most severe impact with its negative influence on the society is nothing, but the diminishing Socialism the return of which, will be the only solution to the malady of this terrifying situation. Dr. Wayne. W. Dyer in his famous work, *Manifest your Destiny (Dyer 1997)* speaks of the diverse stages through which an individual passes in his life time, and Robin S. Ngangom through his poetry points out the diverse stages in the life of female executing different functions at different occasions assuming the roles of a daughter, woman, wife, mother and even a grandmother and along with it he points to the multifaceted existence of man in the contemporary society with the burden of the everyday life. Robin S. Ngangom's poetry, never pursuant to the traditional or conventional norms, speaks of the barefaced realities of life and thus divulges the hidden and hitherto unknown things regarding social life. Robin S. Ngangom, as a poet has higher concern for Socialism, which according to him may function as a stanchion in keeping safe and steady the social structure and thus will lead to a state of harmonious existence when all the socio-cultural, economic or political or even gender biases would come to an extinction to establish a socialist society where the female is neither superior nor inferior to the male. Thus Robin S. Ngangom's poetry is a prophecy of the future.

Temsula Ao, Monalisa Changkija and Robin S. Ngangom have contributed valuably in their poems the burning question of stabilizing a mayhem region, in need of humane feelings and progression, and a better co-existence, thus in keeping with the 21st century in all its needs, wants and achievements. The three poets, have recognized that there are many problems in society today, which are a source of conflict and violence, and so by way of writing poetry, have dedicated themselves, working near and far, day in day out, to building that peaceful society, for man and all around him, to live in joy and peace.

2
Theory of Socialism and Feminism

1. Socialism

William Ebenstein rightly says, that it is not easy to state when and where Socialism first appeared. Some sociologists and historians are of the view that it was in Plato's *Republic* (*Mahajan 2003:691*) that Socialism first appeared there are others, who trace its origin to the Old Testament of *The Holy Bible (Nelson1987)*. The *Bible* is suffused with a universality appeal which has placed it, at the head and the foundation of modern literature. It deals with the origin of the world and man, in which everyone is interested. It emphasizes the conception that all nations are of one blood and that all men are brethren, because God alone is the creator of all. The moral of the *Bible* is addressed to the well being of all human beings in the world. It also deals with the future of mankind and it proclaims the glory of God. '*The Psalter,* the most lyrical part of the *Bible* is perhaps the widest in its appeal, because it echoes the devout feelings of every believing soul in the world. It is a great classic that has exerted and is exerting great influence on human thought and mankind. The religious sentiments of the community appear in various forms, charged with sincerity and passion.' *(Nelson 1987: 476-534).*

The elements of Socialism can also be traced back to pre-historic times. Inequalities must have been a part of human life ever since man began to live in groups. But as a movement Socialism originated much later. The Renaissance and Reformation was a revival of protest against inequalities based on wealth. However, the conclusion of Ebenstein that Socialism as a major force originated out of Capitalism holds true, a philosophy that has given an impetus to the spirit of reform.

As it is understood today, Socialism emerged as a reaction to the rise and development of Capitalism. There is a growing destructive tendency to use the terms Socialism and Communism interchangeably. Communism is only a variety of Socialism, which is a larger concept. Generally speaking Socialism is the political and economic principle, that community as whole should have ownership and control of all means of production and distribution. Socialism can be defined as, the collective ownership and democratic management of the social means of production for the common good. We use the general term "collective", rather than some more specific term because common ownership under Socialism will no doubt take on various forms like national, state, municipal, labor-union and cooperative. The term 'democratic management' is used in the given definition because collectivism without democracy would not be Socialism. We have adopted the term 'social means' of production instead of 'all means' as all socialists agree many kinds of small industry will probably be left in private hands. It is the large-scale industries in which labor is performed socially, by groups or masses of men working with tools owned by other men, that socialists insist should be made collective property. And finally, we say the "common good" rather than the "equal good" or some other term which assumes foreknowledge of the rule of recompense for labour or service in the society of the future.

Socialism strives for the "greatest good of the greatest number" but no one today can say upon what basis the apportioning of that goodwill is determined. It is evident that in the definition selected Socialism is considered as a social ideal, a proposed or anticipated system of society. But the word “Socialism” has a breadth, and inclusiveness, which has many meanings. Socialism may be regarded, as a theory of social evolution, as a system of political economy, as an organized international movement, as a social ideal, or in a usage somewhat loose and vague, but necessary from a genetic or historical standpoint, as a spirit, a passion, an aspiration with its resulting effort, for industrial equality. Contemporary writers use the word in the sense of any of the definitions given or broadly and comprehensively in a sense including all of them. Karl Marx (1818-1883), Auguste Comte (1798-1857) and Herbert Spencer (1820-1903), were three of the great masters of sociological thought. Karl Marx was a socialist theoretician and organizer, a major figure in the history of economic and philosophical thought and a great social prophet. According to Marx society comprised a moving balance of antithetical forces that generate social change by their tension and struggle. For him, struggle rather than peaceful growth was the engine of progress. Strife was the father of all things, and social conflict the core of historical process. Every positive economic change in the society is brought about by the class struggle between the haves and have-nots. The economic, social, political and religious crisis paved the way for the class struggles in which great writers of all ages have participated carrying the mightiest weapon ever used -The Pen. Marx was no exception. He was a prolific writer and a great philosopher. Marx missed the head of the nail, when he failed to realize the fact that the economic equality envisaged by communism, (himself) would remain as a utopian reality, as long as intellectual disparity existed. History proves that an intelligently unequal race cannot become socially or economically equal. The intelligentsia has always been exploiting the intelligently backward. According to Laveleye,

> Socialism has rendered a real service by calling attention to the evils and inequities of the existing social order and by awaking in the hearts of all good men the desire to apply a remedy.
>
> (*Mahajan 2003:697*)

Socialism promotes social welfare, because it emphasizes on society, not on individuals, thereby providing equal opportunities to all. The aim of Socialism is man's emancipation, his restoration to the un-alienated, un-crippled individual, who enters into a new rich spontaneous relationship with his fellowmen and nature. The vast expansion of a progressive theory, a hallmark of the 21st Century, that advocated a departure from the past which in the view point of the proponents of rapid progress, a backward pulling force, an a farsighted glance into the future, which is diagnosed as the first symptoms of an incessant progressive culture, resulted in the entry and re-entry of a series of arguments and the resultant affirmation of theoretical conclusions, in almost every substrata of the society, irrespective of the status which people enjoyed, regarding caste, creed culture or finance in that particular social system.

The subterranean currents running through each society, in different forms and which mostly may be uncharted in the very peripheral level of existence but sometimes working from within often in the deep invincible structure of a society, like a cancerous encroachment, after the attitudinal cohesion giving way to counter theoretical challenges which in turn may ginger the argumentative temperament leading to an uprooted social stability. It is adversarial strands in the process of a social existence, experienced by many in many a social situation, tearing them apart into an existence in a 'no man's land', finally, culminating in their exile from everyman's land in to a state of a non-existent, have to be entwined, of course not with exerted force but with a process of reconciliation if the much awaited dream of many, that of Socialism is to be a reality. In the words of Jawaharlal Nehru,

> I must frankly confess that I am a Socialist...I recognize however, that it may not be possible for a body constituted... to adopt a full Socialistic programme. We must realize that the philosophy

> of Socialism has gradually permeated the entire structure of society. /We talk about our Five Year Plans, about economics, industrialization, progress and freedom. They are all highly important. But ... the real progress of a country means progress not only on the political, economic plane. They have to be integrated, all these, when a nation goes forward.
>
> *(Bhardwaj, 2006:173, 189)*

The intangible nature of the concept, Socialism, though passed through the hands of many a generation for a delicate but definite, definition still evades all the possibilities of a very concrete form of explanation or rather definition. A socialist atmosphere, considered being highly conclusive to the proper growth and functioning, was the ever cherished dream of any nation or any group of people or in other words any where there is a social life or a society. Many ideas and ideologies finding its birth at one time or other in the course of history had made its landmarks in the lives of the people, but while other ideas has only a skin- deep importance and significance in the lives of the people, Socialism, ever since its inception in the minds of the people, never experienced a setback, rather in the occurrence of the uncongenial social situations one ardently wishes for the relief provided by Socialism.

Socio-cultural communities with all their characteristic features, while populating a specific geographic region demonstrates at least some glimpses of the socialist element and even where anarchy or autonomy is the reigning spirit, there too one may visualize the glimmering socialist elements in the insufferable atrocities under which their lives are sandwiched. The sardonic and stipulated norms, whether they are religious, political, cultural or social intended to oppress a group gradually results in the extinction of the socialist concept. The distorted picture of the society, due to the rat race of the day for material progress and the impositions of steadfast laws and dictates lacking in the flexibility for a progress or change, can be redrawn with the confirmed adaptation of the socialist framework, which is a fashion and synthesis of a series of things, situations and events where the boundaries drawn in favour of a peculiar group fades from vicinity, thus formulating the extension of the field of social existence. The outmoded concepts of the past, which at one time in the past experienced a total bloom, in accordance with the demands of the day, gradually turn to the socialist pattern, which is not an ordained or imposed order of things rather one situation borne out of the conglomeration of the allied view points and temperamental aspects of a social group. The petty prejudices of one social group concerning, may be members of the same social group or that of another social or cultural group, warps the physical, social, cultural, economic, psychological and even spiritual or moral frame of the 'subaltern' culture became perpetual oppressions disorganizes the totality of that particular culture. Even in a situation like that of 'real politic', there can also be a chance for Socialism to exist because it is not merely the moral or economic yardsticks with which one assesses and evaluates, Socialism rather it is a term which even crosses the terrains of a society or the social group.

The namby-pamby speculations or the sentimental or the cynical outlooks on Socialism may reach a conclusion as to view it a hindrance to the rapid, racy progress of the society especially on materialistic matters, but a prismatic crystal clear penetration into the core of Socialism would reveal to one, the upper hand that it can gain over any other theories, ideals or ideologies as Socialism paves the way not merely for the individual growth but a collective growth through which the individual integrity, never putting at stake, is sustained and his growth is ensured. In a socialist society, the term Socialism has only a scant relevance due to the process of upliftment and standardization that goes on there in a perpetual manner, in which both the poor and the rich may share the same footing, on the socialist mode of existence and the term synthesis may be of higher significance on the sharing of a series of experiences, along with even the psychic dimensions are made possible in Socialism.

Thus, a socialist society has transformed itself into a 'bogland' where everything fuses into one single substance of a specific quality, with the delicacy and softness. Seamus Heaney, the Irish poet of the "Bogland" speaks of such a bogland situation in the poem "Bogland" and here one may be able to view a strange Socialism:

> They'll never dig coal here
> Only the waterlogged trunks
> Of great firs soft as pulp
> Our pioneers keep striking
> Inwards and downwards
> Every layer they strip
> Seems camped on before
> The bogholes might be atlantic seepage
> The wet centre is bottomless

The depth of Socialism is equal to that of the wet centre of the bogland that becomes the consciousness of history as the preserved things of the bogland, reminds one of the historical past. The flexibility of the bogland to contain and sustain anything in it without causing much harm, can be found even in Socialism, which in a way becomes a byword for sustenance and survival. The deadening effects of the conflicts in the contemporary society can be, in an effective manner, evicted by the installation of Socialism, which is a feather on the euphony of the social life. The residual elements of prehistoric violence and barbarity through a process of evolution, expresses itself to the highest degree possible in modern times where political aspirations as well as social, cultural and ethnic dreams speak through the voice of violence. In this context of bitterness and scathing antagonism, a voice has to emerge to draw the attention of the factions that are engaged in the perpetual war, into the power of Socialism and here literature finds itself to be duly bound in carrying out this function of the 'voice' and often, even through 'silence', literature does a lot of Socialism and for Socialism.

Socialism, to be a reality, must be sequential to the level of functioning forward without an arbitrary pause, while encountering the difficulties, only in a socialist pattern of the society. Where distinctions and demarcations are hardly ever made, hostilities and antagonisms disappear and where the individual effort put together forming a 'collectivist' formula orient towards social regeneration can supersede welfare over wastage and be made a reality.

There is no other country in the world that offers as astounding variety in virtually every aspect of social life as India. Diversities of ethnic, linguistic, economic, religious, class and caste groups crosscut Indian society, which is also permeated with immense urban rural differences, and gender distinctions. Significant differences are found, in the day to day activities of the people, living in different regions of India- especially North, South and North-East. Yet, amid the complexities of Indian life, widely accepted cultural themes enhance social harmony and order. Synthesis of different cultures is the tradition of India. In her long history of thousands of years, India has not rejected any culture; instead she has imbibed the different cultures and made them a part of her own vast culture. The greatest advantage for the modern Indian society is that the motherland has not compromised on the values of the different cultures she has accepted. Even in the modern times India is a hierarchical society, whether in North or North-East India, Christian or Hindu, urban or village, virtually all things, people or social groups are ranked according to various essential qualities. Societal hierarchy is evident in India by a mere perusal of the different caste groups. The general behaviour of an individual is shaped by his knowledge of the social class and cast group to which he belongs. Hierarchy plays an important role within families, and kinship groupings also. Age differences are recognized, and elders are respected in all social groups.

Whether in the ancient, medieval or modern times, India has always been a socially interdependent society. Social interdependence is one of the great themes pervading Indian life. Everyone in India is born into groups-families, clans, sub-castes, castes and religious communities and is nurtured with a deep sense of inseparability from these groups. People identify each other with different groups. For many Indians, the greatest fear is the possibility of being left alone, without social support. Instances of people being chased out from their homes, and even from the villages are common in India, even in the 21st Century. Psychologically, family members typically experience intense emotional interdependence. I, my, we, our, are terms relevant to every individual. Almost in every activity social ties help a person and the absence of them bring failure. In the rapidly modernizing India the traditional joint household remains for most Indians the primary social force, in both ideal and practice. The rich and vibrant culture of India is transmitted from generation to generation primarily through the families. The joint family system is highly valued, ideally consisting of several generations residing, working, eating and worshiping together. Large families tend to be flexible and well suited to modern Indian life, especially for the more than two-thirds of Indians who are involved in agriculture. With the commencement of the post-modern era there occurred a change in the family set up in India, i.e. the arrival of the nuclear families - a couple with their unmarried children - but belong to strong networks of beneficial kinship ties. Arrival of the European powers to India has resulted in India accepting the European cultures. The idea of the nuclear family arrived in India with the arrival of the Europeans.

One of the most distinguishing features of the modern Indian society is the class system and the social inequality based on the class system that is prevalent. Social inequality exists through out the world, but perhaps nowhere has inequality been as elaborately constructed as in the Indian institution of caste. Varna, Caste and other divisions have existed for many centuries, but in the modern period, it has been severely criticized and is undergoing significant changes. Rabindranath Tagore has rightly pointed out in his *Gitanjali* that India, has been broken up into fragments:

> Where the mind has not been broken up into fragments
> by narrow domestic walls
> Where words come out from the depth of truth
> Where tireless striving stretches its arms towards perfection;
>
> *(Edacheriparambil, 1990:14)*

Different tribes, languages, castes, religions are all factors that divide India. The pain that the poets undergo seeing their motherland ruthlessly being hurt, by her own children is mirrored in many of the poems from the region. The word 'caste' is derived from the Portuguese 'Casta', meaning species, race, or kind. Among Indian terms sometimes translated as caste are varna, jati, jat, and samaj. Varna or color actually refers to four large categories (Bhrahmin, Kshatriya, Vaishya and Shudra) that include numerous castes. The other terms refer to castes and subdivisions of castes often called sub-castes. There are thousands of castes and sub-castes in India involving hundreds of millions of people. In India membership in castes is achieved by birth. Çaste membership provides a sense of belonging to a recognized group from whom support can be expected in a variety of situations. There are a number of castes which are still associated with traditional occupations, such as priests, potters, barbers, carpenters, leatherworkers, butchers and launderers. Members of higher ranking castes tend to be more prosperous than members of lower-ranking castes, who often endure poverty and social disadvantage. Those citizens of India whom Gandhiji fondly called 'Harijans' or

'Children of God' are known as 'Scheduled Castes' they were considered as 'Untouchables' prior to 1935. Today, the correct terms for these groups, who make up about 16% of the population, is Dalit, or 'oppressed'. Other groups, usually called tribes (often referred to as 'Scheduled Tribes') are also integrated into the caste system to varying degrees. In the modern India too, Dalits in certain areas have to display extreme difference to high status people and are barred from most temples and wells. Such degrading discrimination was outlawed under legislation passed during British rule and was repudiated by pre-independence reform movements led by Mahatma Gandhi and Bhimrao Ramji Ambedkar, a Dalit leader. After Independence in 1947, Dr. Ambedkar single handedly wrote India's Constitution, including provisions barring caste based discrimination. However, Dalits as a group still suffer significant disadvantages, especially in rural areas. Rapid economic progress and spread of education have brought about an awareness regarding the equality of human beings among the citizens. Still in rural areas, many low- caste people suffer from landlessness, unemployment, and discriminatory practices. In most of the growing cities, caste affiliations are often unknown to casual associates and traditional restrictions on inter-caste interactions are fading fast. A large number of Indians reside in villages, where caste and class affiliations overlap. Large landholders are overwhelmingly upper caste, and small scale farmers belong to the middle castes, while landless laborers typically belong to the lowest ranking castes. These groups tend to form a three-level class system of stratification in rural areas, and members of the groups are drawing together within regions across caste lines, in order to enhance their economic and political power.

When looking at the modern Indian society as a whole, defining classes is a difficult task, rife with vague standards. An astonishing fact is that the upper classes include only about one percent of the total population or nearly ten million people, encompassing wealthy property owners, industrialists, former royalty, top executives and prosperous entrepreneurs. Slightly below them are the many millions of the upper middle class. At the other end of the scale is more than half of India's population, including low-level workers of many kinds, as well as hundreds of millions of extremely poor people, who endure grossly inadequate housing and education and many other economic hardships. Ambitious politicians ruthlessly exploit this large population. A number of Indians have surmounted to a comparatively new class known to the Indian society as the middle-class. The surreptitious money-making attitudes of the politicians and the upper classes have not prevented the rapid expansion of a prosperous middle class. Estimated at perhaps 300 million people - more than the entire population of the US - this new vanguard, straddling town and countryside and all religious communities, is mobile, driver, and consumer-oriented and to some extent forward looking. This group includes prosperous farmers, white-collared workers, business and professional people, military personnel and a multitude of others all enjoying decent homes, reasonable incomes inclusive of educated and healthy children.

An understanding of the village structure and urban life is important, in order to fully understand the great literature that has bloomed and is continuing to flourish in India. About three-fourths of India's people live in some 500,000 villages, where the most basic business of India- Agriculture, takes place. Most of the villages have fewer than 1,000 inhabitants, but some have as many as 5,000 people. Indian villages are often quite complex and are not isolated socially or economically. Residents of these villages typically range from priests and cultivators to merchant, artisans and laborers. Traditionally, villages often recognize a headman (not a woman) and a Panchayat, a council composed of important local men. Normally, disputes were adjudicated within the village, with infrequent recourse to the police or courts. Today, the government supports an elective Panchayat and headman system, which is distinct from the traditional system, and in many cases, mandates the inclusion of members who are women or very low caste.

The most important factor that is affecting the transformation of Indian Society is the acceleration of urbanization. More than 25% of the country's population is urban. Most of the large cities of India are densely populated, congested, noisy polluted, and deficient in clean water, electricity, sanitation and decent housing. Slums abound, often cheek by jowl with luxury apartment buildings, with the roads overrun with pedestrians, cattle, and vehicles spewing diesel fumes. A pleasant fact about Indian city life is that, caste hierarchies are weak in cities, but the caste status remains important, as scarce jobs are often obtained through caste fellows, relatives and friends. Ingenuity and tenacity characterize poor urban workers supporting themselves through a multitude of tasks as entrepreneurs, petty traders and menial laborers. Indian cities, just like any other great cities of the world, are the great hubs of commerce, education, science and politics upon which the functioning of the nation depends.

The greatest visible changes in the Indian life came about in the modern era not in the field of politics and institutions, but in the unprecedented acceleration of economic development and its influence on life-styles, modes of consumption, sexual codes, personal relationships and individual expectations. Life became more modern. The entire codes that very strictly regulated the way of living of the Indians underwent a sea change. Familial and sexual changes were observed with great concern among the different social classes, who began to look back nostalgically to the stability of the social system, that existed in the previous age as the institution of marriage and family witnessed a total change during this period. The private as well as the public dynamics of the social life changed. These social revolutions, receive the support of urban visionaries, shaping the growing literary movement in India.

A mere look at the most popular and award winning books of the past three decades will reveal the fact, that writers in India are very much concerned, with the social changes that are taking place in India. Sahitya Akademi Awards were conferred for excellence in poetic literature to the following poets: Jayant Mahapatra *Relationship (1981)*, Nissim Ezekiel *Latter-Day Psalms (1983)*, K.N. Daruwalla *The Keeper of the Dead (1984)*, Kamala Das *Collected Poems (1985)* and Shiv kumar *Trapfalls in the Sky (1987)*.Futhermore, *The God of Small Things (1997)* by Arundhati Roy, *Inheritance of Loss (2006)* by Kiran Desai, and the most recent *White Tiger (2008)* by Aravind Adiga, are some of the award winning books dealing with the present or past social issues and are intended to bring about social changes. Justice in matters pertaining to class, gender, and access to desirable resources, in the past and at the present times, remains an elusive goal of the social thinkers in India.

As Alexander Solzhenitsyn declared,

> Literature that is not the breath of contemporary society that dare not transmit the pains and fears of that society that does not warn in time against threatening moral and social dangers- such literature does not deserve the name of literature; it is only a façade.
>
> *("Open Letter to the Forth Soviet Writers Congress" 16th. May 1967).*

2. Feminism

Feminism is not a science or philosophy. In common parlance Feminism is known as a movement of women, by women, and for women to achieve women's rights. It is also known as women's liberation movement. The term 'Feminism' was first used by the French dramatist Alexander Dumas the younger, in 1872 in a pamphlet *'L Homme- Femme'* to designate the – then emerging movement for women's rights. It gradually emerged to be a worldwide cultural movement, to secure complete equality of women with men, in the enjoyment of all human rights. Feminist criticism started as a revolt against male domination. Initially the movement was mainly a strong protest against man-made morality, andro-centric culture and discrimination between man and woman in society and literature.

The history of Feminism can be divided into three 'waves'. The first wave refers mainly to women's suffrage movements of the 19th and early 20th centuries. This was mainly concerned with women's enfranchisement. The second 'wave' refers to the ideas and actions associated with women's liberation movements beginning in the nineteen sixties. It was the Feminist Liberals assertion for women. Their argument merged with liberalism's assumption that one God sets natural process in motion, and all objects, including minds are governed, by law discovered by human reason. They argue that women's mind are formed in nature like men's - free to find truth. The third wave refers to a continuation of, and reaction to, the perceived failures extend from the 1990's to the present. Feminist theory can be said to have emerged from these feminist movements. It manifests through a variety of disciplines such as feminist geography, feminist history and feminist literary criticism. Feminist criticism can be divided into two varieties:

(1) The first type is concerned with woman as reader, absorbing the literature produced by a male dominated society. This is called feminist critique, and it includes the images and stereotypes of women in literature, the omissions and false ideas about women in criticism and the exploitation of female audience.

(2) The second type of feminist criticism is concerned with woman as writer, as the producer of history

and themes. Its subject includes female creativity, female language, female literary history and studies of particular writers and works and is called Gynocritics. (*Channa 2004.34-35*). One of the problems of the feminist critique is that it is male-oriented. Readers are told of the limited roles women play in literary history, or rather what men wanted women to be. The feelings and experiences of women are hardly mentioned. The critique's resistance to questioning is increased and she develops a tendency to naturalize women's victimization. On the other hand, Gynocritics refuse to accept male models and theories. They snap their links with male literary tradition, and focus on the world of female culture. Feminism has succeeded in altering predominant perspectives, in a wide range of areas within western society, ranging from culture to law. Feminist activists have campaigned for women's legal rights, for rights of bodily integrity and autonomy, for protection from domestic violence, sexual harassment and rape, for work place rights. Feminist activists have stood against all forms of discrimination. Most of the leaders of the feminist movements had been middle class white women, from Western Europe and North America. By the middle of the 19th century, women of other races had proposed alternative Feminisms. This trend accelerated in the 1960s with the civil rights movement, in the United States and the collapse of European colonialism in Africa, the Caribbean, parts of Latin America and Southeast Asia. Since that time, women in former European colonies and the third world have proposed 'post colonial' and 'third world' Feminism. Western feminists were criticized for being ethnocentric by postcolonial feminists.

Clara Zetkin was one of the prominent feminist of the Marxist era. Besides being a leading activist she subsequently became a founder member of the German Communist Party, but in 1921 took charge of the Communist International Women's Secretariat and spent most of the rest of her life in the Soviet Union. However, soon after the Bolshevik Revolution, Lenin admonished her for encouraging women members of the Communist Party to discuss sexual matters, rather than the fact that the 'first state of proletarian dictatorship is battling with the counter-revolutionaries of the whole world.' Of still greater significance was Alexandra Kollantai, who had written the *Social Bases of the Woman Question* in 1980 before fleeing Russia for Western Europe. After her return to Russia, she played an active role in the Bolshevik Revolution, and in 1920 she headed a special department within the Communist Party devoted to women's issues. In this period she continue to write about the socialist relationship between women and men, advocating complete abolition of existing family structures, in favour of heterosexual love base on attraction and a joint commitment to creating a new society.

There are many senses in which the sprawling edifice of modern Feminism can be considered as built on the foundations laid by Simone de Beauvoir in the *Second Sex (1949)* wherein she states,

> This has always been a man's world, and none of the reasons that have been offered in explanation have seemed adequate.
>
> *(Davies. 2006: 122)*

Beauvoir's analysis of women, subordination proceeded from the assumption, that men viewed women as fundamentally different from themselves, and in being defined as 'the other' women were reduced to the status of the 'second sex'. Her book deplored the oppression of women who, she argued, had been thwarted throughout history by the generally accepted view that men were the norm and women an aberration from it. She claimed that history, myth and literature reinforced the idea of women as an inferior sex and rejected the idea that the male ideal was the only one to which women could aspire. These were ideas that Beauvoir confronted and inspired women to take control of their lives. Humanity is male, and woman is defined not in herself but as relative to man, never as an autonomous being. She is the incidental, inessential as opposed to the essential or the basic. Many of the best known writings of this second wave of Feminism came to be seen as a set of variations of this theme.

In the *Second Sex*, as stated earlier, Beauvior's analysis begins from the assumption, that man has always seen 'woman' as the other. But there can be no presence of the other in the real sense unless the 'other' is recognized as a consciousness, which is both separate and also identical with the 'self'. In this sense the other seen both as the subject and also as the object. But since the earliest day of the patriarchy, man has always seen woman only as 'object'. He is not prepared to let woman become 'subject'. Because women have never set themselves up as 'subject', they have never projected myths of their own. A myth always implies a subject who projects his hopes and fears towards a 'sky of transcendence,' women still dream through the dreams of men. But as man's 'inessential other', the woman herself has become 'a myth', the myth of woman as created by man. This 'myth of woman' will not end, until women assert themselves as human beings. At the root of many 'myths about women' there lie the ambivalent feelings of security, and fear in man who sees the woman as his other and also Nature. He is both born of her, and also dies in Nature's laps. Since man, the absolute spirit has to yield to nature or woman, man suffers from a guilt complex. He is haunted by the fear that in-yielding to the powers of woman who represents flesh, man has become a sinner. This mixed feeling toward woman, has generated several myths about child-bearing, side of the woman in many tribal societies. Every aspect of child bearing is associated with the feeling of impurity. The girl remains impure during the days of her menstruation. There are several other woman myths. Women have the power to hear mysterious voices; she can communicate with birds and spirits. She is an expert palm reader. The dead men and Gods speak through her mouth. Man created these myths because subconsciously he saw woman as source of danger and she inspired terror in man.

A new type of myth came into existence with the birth of Christianity. Woman's figure has become spiritualized. She has become the soul of the group, the city and the nation (Virgin Mary). The emotions of pity and tenderness have been assigned to her. The civilized man want, that his wife should surrender herself completely to him. Since the coming of the patriarchal regime, man has become the master of woman. Man began to find in woman bright stars and a dreaming moon. This was the result of making woman property of a single man. It was only then that she was regarded as an object of beauty. In the Nazi Germany and in ancient Sparta, women were for the state and not for the individual. So in these societies woman was not adored for her duty. Even in the modern society we expect the woman to accept her husband's 'point of view'. She should yield to his arguments as coming from a superior intellect. Her body is meant for the gratification of his sexual thirst. In love-making, man is the supposed initiator. He makes all important decisions. Woman has no right to question him.

Feminism, as a term can be considered as an all inclusive term where even the male sensibility doesn't find itself out of place and as a concept this was of heated arguments and debates not only in the literary scenario rather the socio-cultural discourses, once amputated due to certain 'absences', found a new energy and reciprocal recognitions due to the advent of this into the discussions of contemporary life. A good number of critics and theoreticians along with the practitioners of Feminism, literary output as well as in the social practices and behavior tried to disentangle the complex web of Feminism in order to deprive it of the mythical aura or the prejudicial propagandas made against it, and they believed that once the actualities and the core of what Feminism is concretized in the minds of the ordinary men, the emancipation of the female will be at hand as reality is made to break out of the thick walls created around it can juxtapose the arguments of Feminism with the contemporary reality. The "second sex" and "the other", from the beginning of the historical exodus to a state of civilization, had to face the bitter experience of a suppression, manifesting itself in different forms and through which, in the course of time, they gradually identified themselves with the arduous tasks and the roles bestowed on them and thus the history of the female is one of a great anguish.

The ever increasing intricacy of the social structure and the automatised existence of the individual is such a fragmented and withered social climate, could make it impact very seriously felt in the momentum with which life moves forward here we see, in the lap of modernity - the streptococcus of the day- the fluency of life got lost and everywhere, when one turns for a consolation, what he embarks on is nothing but new problems germinating out of the novel policies of the day.

Women's writing has proved itself, without a tinge of hesitation, to be one of the very major instruments in the propagation of the female sensibility. Virginia Woolf's *A Room of One's Own (1929),* is a classic document of the Feminist Movement. Besides, Betty Friedan's *The Feminine Mystique (1963)*, is become a bestseller book that reflects, what really is in the air about Feminism. A woman's sensibility manifests itself in the arrogonality in a woman's text and rereading has to be made of these texts in a biological, linguistic, psychoanalytic and cultural formats. The metaphorical implications of female biological difference in writing especially finding expression in the form of an anxiety about the lack of the phallic authority, and that which was seen with a suspicious eye by the patriarchy , gets a complete negation in the feminist criticism. As far as a female is concerned, this sexual differentiation, rather than becoming a limitation, should act as a resource rather than a destiny as against the patriarchal notions which have limited the female biology to its own narrow specifications. In the feminist discourses often the 'absences" or the 'lack' experienced by the 'other' turns out to be instrumental in the justification of the masculine power which nails the female to a narrow confined space, where the circumference of a woman's world, day by day, because narrower finally culminating in her being tied to a peg of masculine intentions and impulsive instincts out of which the female identity wound be largely defined in terms of a 'taboo transgressor' and thus becoming an outcast. The circumscription of each woman, who has a peculiar psychological pattern beyond the complete grasp of the male, eats at the face of her a series of traumatic experiences and while pressed against the wall of suppression to an extent where tolerance is no more a reality which can be advocated, breaks open the doors of rage and there may follow the gush of emotions as an avalanche. This unsurpassed expression of anger and frustration of a female against a male is seen in "Daddy" by Sylvia Plath:

> Of I've killed one men, I've killed two-
> The vampire who said he was you
> And drank my blood for a year
> Seven graces, of you want to know
> Daddy, you can lie back now
> There's a stake on your fat black heart
> And the villages never liked you
> They are dancing and stamping on you
> They always knew it was you
> Daddy, Daddy you bastard I'am though.

Even the linguistic expression of a male and the female is taken for consideration and conclusions are drawn regarding the problems of women's use of language and an analysis of this issue becomes part of the gyno-criticism. Even in the field of language and literature, the very mark of the dominant mode of discourse shows the mark of the dominant masculine ideology and thus the expressive instincts of the female too undergoes an oppression and she is forced to speak in a language with which she feels really uncomfortable, because for her it is not the genuine expression of herself. Therefore the dominant tendency found among women is to be silent or speechless, where she is placed outside the historical process experiencing the existence of an alienated being, just because that history has always been defined in male centered terms. In order to rectify such as awkward darkness, especially experience by the female, we must, for a time, focus on a women- centered inquiry, considering the possibility of an existing female culture over, or even within the general culture which is a patriarchal, male centered culture but in outward appearance shared by both male and female. Feminism, as a term of higher significance in the contemporary society focuses its attention primarily on the 'woman's culture', which according to the patriarchal viewpoints denote or even stand as a 'sub culture' where the heightened model of sub standardization works on par with the preconceived notions that have been developed by the male. The female culture and tradition have its own power and weaknesses revealing itself in the form of higher out puts and the highest mode of resistance and at the same time expressing the powerlessness for sustenance. Thus Feminism is a complex and complicating theme, dealing not merely with one aspect of the female, rather it is an attempt of recovery – of the female and 'the Feminism'.

Feminism in the Indian context is a by-product of the western liberalism in general and feminist thought in particular. The indigenous contributing factors have been the legacy of equality of sexes inherited from the freedom struggle, constitutional right of women, spread of education and the consequent new awareness among women. The Indian woman is caught in the flux of tradition and modernity; but both cast off their aspirations. One of the newly accepted trends in the modern Indian society is the tendency to break up relationships established through marriages. With the divorce of the couples, the relatives also come to hostile terms. Divorce was not a practice either in ancient or medieval India, but in the modern Indian society there are a few practices as common as divorce.

Hindu and Muslim women follow complex rules of veiling the body and avoidance of public appearance, especially before relatives linked by marriage and before strange men. Purdah practices are linked to patterns of authority and harmony within the family. Hindu and Muslim Purdah observances differ in certain key ways, but female modesty and decorum as well as concepts of family honour, and prestige are essential to the various forms of Purdah. Purdah restrictions are generally stronger for women of conservative high status families. The superiority of the husband had been established and his deification by the wife had come into vogue fully by the end of the post Vedic era. Practices like Sati and female infanticide exist even in the modern Indian society of the 21st century. The birth of an infant is celebrated with rites of welcome and blessing typically much more elaborate for a boy than for a girl. The 2001 census counted only 933 females per 1000 males, reflecting sex-selective abortion, poorer medical care and nutrition, and occasional infanticide targeting females. Most of the parents in India, favour boys because of their value in agricultural activities tend to be higher, and after marriage a boy continues residing with his parents, supporting them as they age. Boys ought to look after their parents in their old age. In contrast a girl drains family resources, especially when a large dowry goes with her to her husband's home. In recent decades, demands for dowry have become quite exorbitant in certain groups.

Historically, one of the special features of ancient Indian culture was that women had always constituted an educated, cultured and respected limb of the society inseparable from it. On examining the status of women in the Rig Vedic age, one understands that women enjoyed freedom to the highest degree. They would participate in the performance of sacrifice with men so much that no Yajna was considered to be complete without the active participation of women, called 'Ardhangini'. Many a learned and scholarly women Rishis and sages are mentioned in the Rig Vedic literature. Lopamudra, Urvashi, Ghosha and Apala are only a few of them. There was no restriction on women receiving education in the age of Upanishads. There were highly educated women who undertook the duty of teaching in the Upanishads. In the period of Sutras too women were not prohibited from receiving education, or actively participating in the different social activities. Women were even admitted to military training as indicated by the word 'Shaktiki' used by Patanjali which means a female spear-bearer. Thus it becomes evident, that no major distinction was made in the number of opportunities, applicable of men and that of women. In the post-Vedic period too women were highly respected and honored. They had full freedom to develop their personality. But as time passed, things began to change. During the Buddhist and Mughal periods men were considered superior to women. Women were best thought of, as the mistress of the household. The women folk remained comparatively educationally backward during these periods.

Today, the constitution of India, as mentioned in its preamble guarantees every citizen the fundamental right to equality. Yet after 60 years of Independence, just one perusal of the female infant mortality figures, the literacy rates and the employment opportunities for women is sufficient evidence that discrimination exists. This gender bias is evident in every walk of life. Never has women's representation in the Indian Parliament been more than 10 percent. One of the rapidly vanishing yet significant aspects of Indian family life is Purdah or the veiling and seclusion of women, which was brought about by the

Mohammedans in much of the North and Central India, and some parts of the South and North-East India.

Women found a new identity in the Indian social scenario, where the concept of a 'Victorian mother' has been erased by the emergence of the 'new woman'. As per the changing sensibilities, there began an attempt to redefine the boundaries, between the private and public social roles of a woman. In the field of literature, which has been highly prosperous during this era, there were earnest attempts to redraw the values, social systems and above all the concept of womanhood. Writers were the dissectors, of psychological peculiarities and disintegrating social systems, became prominent figures in this respect. In creative genius, in the ability to construct a world of imagination in which reality is more accessible, than it is in the everyday activities of life, these writers have few peers in modern Indian English Literature. These poems are an angry, fearful and yet compassionate, a chronicle of the troubled flow of and confluence of the writers' emotions and of the resultant agency of an existential dilemma. How there takes place a rape of the women's psyche by terrific, all encompassing socio-cultural structures is dealt with, in most of these works. Feminism today is thematic in Indian literature. The literatures of the recent years contribute to a great extent for gender equality.

The Feminist movement in India, largely led by educated urban women, seeks gender justice on a wide variety of issues, focusing particularly on the escalating issue of dowry-related murder of young wives, which number in thousands annually. The overwhelming economic needs of poor female workers are being addressed by organizations such as the Self Employed Women's Association of Ahmedabad. Eminent women leaders have come forward to protect women from under the feet of man, both in urban and in rural areas. In recent times the Government of India has set up a "High Powered Committee of eminent persons and experts to study the Status of Women India to enable the Government to take expeditious action." (*Mukherjee 2009.1)* In literary terms it precipitates in a search for identity and a quest for the definition of the self. In critical practice, it boils down to scrutinize empathetically plight of women characters at the receiving end of human interaction.

R.K. Narayan and Mulk Raj Anand are the early Indian writers in English, who are pre-occupied with feminist concerns especially related with women belonging to middle or lower middle class, their attempt to liberate themselves from the restrictions imposed by the system made up by man and the subsequent problems a women has to face in the Indian cultural context. Most of the novels of R. K. Narayan are concerned with the quest for female identity in men-women relationship. R. K. Narayan's *The Dark Room (1938)*, *The Guide (1958)* and *The Painter of Signs (1976)* are concerned with the quest for female identity. His novel, *The Dark Room* has been called by Narayan himself as an early testament of the women's liberation movement. In the words of Nova Kapadia, *The Dark Room* can cited as the only novel of Narayan in which woman is questioning, however mildly, her traditional role. The novel is a lament on the disharmony of domestic life. The second generation of Indian woman novelists like Nayantara Sahgal, Anita Desai, Shobha De have challenged the male culture that prevails in our country. These women portray the tortured consciousness of the urban middle class woman, who in quest of her identity undergoes a metamorphosis-from a silent sufferer to a hard-core rebel, breaking with age-old and restraining ethics of the male-dominated world. At times, the rebellion of the woman takes the extreme form such as sexual promiscuity and extramarital relations which serve as a device for her to assert 'herself'. These contemporary women authors have, with newer insight, penetrated into the deeper layers of complicated social order of post-independence era. They have been influenced by the feminist mode of thinking in their presentation of the main characters and their relationship with other characters.

Women poets have also deftly poetized, Feminism. Besides Kamala Das, other poets who have revealed varied aspects of social, feminine sensibility were Eunice de Souza, Melanie Silgardo, Monika Varma, Gauri Deshpande, Mamta Kalia, and Malathi Rao. These contemporary poets have explored the themes, attitudes, voices of the mess in society, and the situations and problems faced by women. The poets of North-East India too, have romanced the feminist context in their literature. They believe that women are a part of the establishment and are not 'illegal'. As opined by T.N. Mannen,

> It is time to treat women as equal partners with men in all respect of human activities, because women are outshining men in many areas which were traditionally considered as men exclusive privilege. Women active involvement in the planning and decision making process can surely enrich the society which will accelerate development of not only socio-economic but politically as well. Men have nothing to lose by allowing women to develop and contribute their best for the common good. (*Mannen. 2008:7).*

3. Socialism and Feminism in the Poetry of North-East India

The North-Eastern region of India is an abode of all evils and so there is no wonder why the tender hearts of the socially concerned individuals seek for remedies. Most of the poets from the North-East also accept the view that India is already broken up and the disease has spread across the North-Eastern region.

Temsula Ao, Monalisa Changkija and Robin S. Ngangom are three great poets, committed to the social cause and thereby prosperity in all realms, for the natives of the region. They do nothing but expose the hypocrisy of those in power and the suffering of the people who are born under the influence of an unknown, unlucky star. They are concerned with nothing but the emancipation of their people, who live like the bondmen of the eleventh and twelfth centuries. The historical tensions engraved on the geographical arena of a particular region, will certainly have its first manifestations in the psychological sphere of the people of that region, even though they belong to a later generation far removed from the historical juncture of perpetual conflicts as the bleeding wounds of the past drip blood, as a reminder, on their present day life.

A writer while moving through the debris if these historical devastations, formulating a granary of corpses, gets flabbergasted at the sight of the fracture caused to the identity of a nation, especially to that of its citizens in an attempt to crown Socialism, despising any kind of oppressive autocratic pulses in the social scenario and he fails to avert his attention from this and alternately fulminates at the generative forces of these pricking pictures in the form of poetry making these historical as well as geographical situations, a back drop of his writings. The three poets who even amidst the advances of a counter culture of materialism, which sprang up surreptitiously in the beginning but later affirmed its authority, makes attempts to keep intact the fervor for soil and the natural culture, which according to them is the primeval as well as the primary culture of humanity. But never even once, does their poetry degenerate into eulogistic standard, as he tramples on the hypocritical frame work of society purposefully to make the pugnacious tendencies of such a social system to bow its head before the simplicity of the underprivileged, who may be the 'son's of the soil' whose lives are more akin to the primordial culture of the universe. The 'master culture' often ruling over the subservient, making it menial in the eyes of others, who share the blood of the bedecked social group enjoying all privileges and benefits, comes under close scrutiny in the poetry of Temsula Ao, Monalisa Changkija and Robin S. Ngangom. The cultural miscarriage, resulting from the dominance of one sect and the subversion of an order in the life of a larger population, through the repetitive patterns that it follow, lead to a state of an ill-executed, but self-willed social impotence and even a relentless attempt at the rejuvenation of the social scenario will find nothing but a consequential collapse. The ephemeral encounters, between the warring forces, often used as subterfuges to grab the privileges of the other group temporarily create a bankruptcy of values finally resulting in a confused social state strewn with a number of corpses. This agonizing social situation, which furnishes blockades before social progress at the cost of a socialist pattern of society, brings about a really resinous atmosphere both in the private as well as the public, psychological as well as intellectual life of the people acting out the role of a devastative force creating a greater ruckus, leading people astray.

The poetry of Temsula Ao, Monalisa Changkija and Robin S. Ngangom is an open cry to the 'gone astray', shepherding them back to the fold of a restoration. As Indira Gandhi stated,

> A Society is a Mosaic – like a work of art. It takes many elements, many textures and many colors to give the total effect of strength and vitality.
>
> *(Bhardwaj.2006:140)*.

Temsula Ao, Monalisa Changkija and Robin S. Ngagnom have through their poetry given elements, textures and colors, to promote Socialism and also advocate the essence of Feminism. They have set a trend to follow, in the land, in the street, in the homes, besides a trend with ideas, as how to live considering, what is happening around us. The poets have stood for the acceptance of women's attitude and participation in various social problems because these poets believe that the Second Sex is empowered multi-dimensionally. The three poets agree with Susan B. Anthony, who has rightly commented, "There will never be complete equality until women themselves help to make laws and elect lawmakers." *(Davies. 2006: 66)* Their poetry expresses their sensitivity to feministic issues giving a new language, colour and expression to the importance of feminine physique and psychology, in help shaping better homes and an amiable society.

The selected poems, which are the objects of this study reveals the fact that Temsula Ao, Monalisa Changkija and Robin S. Ngangom have a very few similarities in their approach to poetry. One of the similarities in their poems is that, they are all fed up of the existing social order and have a strong desire to expose the folly of the suppressed, whether they belong to the 'underground' or 'overground'. They want their people to throw away the chains which bind them. Temsula Ao, Monalisa Changkija and Robin S. Ngangom in their poetry have given a consecrated endeavor and an exacting discipline:

> 'Make me thy lyre,
>
> Be thou, Spirit fierce,
>
> My spirit!
>
> my words among mankind!
>
> Be through my lips to unawakened earth.'
>
> *(Hutchinson, (ed).1970: 577)*

Temsula Ao, Monalisa Changkija and Robin S. Ngangom are poets, whose poetry comfort the readers, rather than merely amuse. They live in societies with wounded souls still they do not alienate themselves from the wounded, the neglected, the poor and the downtrodden. These poets reveal more of the environment, of their lives, and other's lives and of the specifics of daily life, including relations with others. They know too well, to handle the romance question of Socialism and Feminism. Their poetry has a rich sense of location and a treat of ordinary life. The poetry of Temsula Ao, Monalisa Changkija and Robin S. Ngangom has the power to heal, the hearts of the masses, because of their artistic credo.

3

Romance of Socialism and Feminism in the Poetic Works of Temsula Ao

1. Socialism in Temsula Ao's Poetry

Temsula Ao is one of the most prolific writers of the North-East India. Her poetry is not mere imitation but creation and so, differs from the works of the other contemporary poets. Each line is created, based on the sensations and impressions received, from the external world. The poet who is galvanized by the horror that has become a way of life in the North-Eastern part of India, receives the external stimuli from the society and then these impressions are shaped, ordered, modified and the opposites are reconciled and harmonized by the imagination of the poet, and in this way her thoughts are converted into poetic creations, that intends to bring about social mobility in turn. There is nothing quite as evocative about life of an individual in the North-East of our country as a few lines from the poetry of Temsula Ao. She occupies a very significant position in the modern Indo-Anglian literature. A silent poet of variety she has to her credit a collection of four volumes:

1. *Songs that Tell (1988)*
2. *Songs that Try to Say (1992)*

3. *Songs of Many Moods* (1995)
4. *Songs from Here and There (2003)*

Temsula Ao is predominantly a socialist writer. Most of her poems are concerned with issues that affect the society. The poet realizes that the female identity as constructed by Indian tradition is demeaning and is a trap. The society has allotted a variety of roles to women who struggle in her attempt to perform these various roles. The modern Indian women have succeeded in breaking away the chain of narrow-mindedness to a large extent. The credit for this should definitely go to brave social activists and writers like Temsula Ao who hold firmly on to the principles that they believe is correct, and ethical. Though there is a pseudo cease-fire existing between the undergrounds and the over-grounds, the minds of the people is not at peace. The poet realizes the reality and reflects it in her poems. The poet thirst for peace is the underlying spirit of all her poems. Social stratification pains the poet. Social inequality is a structural and historical reality observable in diverse forms and in different contexts. So the poet relates social inequality to structure, ideology and behaviour of people. The poet stresses on the fact that political and economic exploitation have crept into every aspect of the society. The poet is also concerned with gender stratification. The ugly realities of rape, wife battering, sexual harassment, etc. illustrate and intensify women's subordinate position in the Indian society. She is of the view that even if women reach economic parity with men, and they win equal representation in the government, genuine equality between the sexes cannot be achieved if these attacks remain as common as they are today. Just as African-Americans are victimized by racism, women suffer from sexism in our society. The poet strongly opposes the theory and practice of sexism, which hold that one sex is superior to the other. Many of her poems showcase gender stratification exceeding all limits.

Songs of Many Moods contain some of Temsula's finest literary creations. The poem "The Empty Coffin" is about a funeral, and yet it cannot be called an elegy because it has all the qualities of a lyric. The poem has six stanzas of irregular meter, written in blank verse and is a satire. The poem has sociological significance. The poet mocks the 21st. century middle-class society, which utilizes every opportunity to show off their importance no matter whether they are attending a wedding party or a funeral service. The poem compels its readers for self-examination by stressing upon the plague that has infected not the human body but the human heart. The niggardliness that has crept into the social life, some of them even in the form of cultural advancement is severely criticized by the poet:

They flocked to the funeral,
All dressed up
As though for a showing.
Many came to gawk
At genuine grief
And some to see
Who else turned up. (*SOMM:* 25)

The poem also satirizes the greed of the relatives of the dead effectively. The materialistic culture that is digging our own grave is brought to light thus:

They lowered the cóffin,
Into the hollowed earth,
And dispersed their different ways
To discuss the Will. (*SOMM* : 25)

The poem entitled "My Hills" voices the poet's concern for the protection of environment. She laments that the sounds and sights, have altered in her hills due to human interfering with the nature. She verbalizes the need to detach oneself, from the materialistic attitude of today, and live in harmony with nature, and doubts whether she has lost the very essence of her hills forever. The time when the birds hummed from all corners is lost, and instead gunshots are heard from every nook and corner of her hills. Each season had its own charm in those days, but now nature looks same in all seasons. The poem has a nostalgic feeling when the poet sings:

> The rivers are running red,
>
> The hillsides are bare
>
> And the seasons
>
> Have lost their magic, (*SOMM:* 49)

She concludes the poem only after saying why things are as they are now. She says emphatically that her people have forgotten their rich tradition, and are running behind a 'gun' culture which they think will bring back what they lost. But she is sure that ultimately things have changed, the way nobody wanted it to be:

> Because
>
> The very essence
>
> Of my hills
>
> Are lost
>
> Forever – (*SOMM:* 49)

A close examination of this poem reveals that the poem has a didactic function to perform and that is, to let us realize that we are the greatest destructive force in nature. Though we lie in the lap of nature, our actions are not in harmony with the nature. There is something strikingly different about the poetry of Temsula Ao. Her poems spring from a deeply felt love for the humanity. Temsula Ao comes by like Nature's help; mankind can set into creation, all that is necessary and life sustaining, thereby live and let live.

She is a poet who can rightly be called the voice of the

21st. century North-East India. The last poem in the collection *Songs that Tell* gives the reason why she keeps on writing, and the reason she ascribes is that poetry simply flows out of her on seeing the stark realities of life. Life in a troubled region amid the gun shots, and the cry of the innocent that touches the heart makes her write:

I will have sung
My last song
When I cease to be
Moved
By a maimed body
And a broken spirit. (*STT:* 61)

Temsula Ao fearlessly addresses what Camus called "the double challenge of truth and liberty" (www.raimes.com/camus2.htm). In her poetry, the reader find between the lines a heart that thirsts for truth and liberty, a heart that loves humanity, a heart that knows the truth and is not afraid to speak it out. Her poetry mirrors the contemporary North-East. The poet laments in "My Hills":

The sounds and sights
Have altered
In my hills. (*SOMM* : 48)

In the past there was a perfect blend between the man and the nature. And she is sure there was perfect harmony into the society in those days, for she says:

Once they hummed
With bird song
And happy gurgling brooks
Like running silver
With shoals of many fish. (*SOMM:* 48)

Though the poet has beautifully exploited the beauty of nature in "My Hills" she is more concerned with the social issues. The contemporary society pains the poet:

But today
I no longer know my hills,
The bird song is gone,
Replaced by the staccato
Of sophisticated weaponry. (*SOMM:* 49)

And she knows the reason for the ill-fate of her people. Not because God has been blind to them but simply:

Because
The very essence
Of my hills
Are lost
Forever. (*SOMM:* 49)

Temsula Ao takes us on a journey into the cosmic nature that lies within the world which man has fragmented. And yet in her poetry she seeks to represent a sense of ecological responsibility. The matter of survival, according to Escamill, "requires a holistic interdependence of person, place, spirit and practice." (*Murphy. 2009: pp 6-7)* The poet has also, paid attention to each and every aspect of the society. Not even "The Beggar" escapes her attention:

I saw the horrid mass
Writhing by the way side
Pushing his battered bowl
towards the pedestrians
In mute supplication. (*SOMM:* 17)

She does not elaborate on the plight of the beggar in

her society, but reveal the attitude of the mass. The mass has no eyes, no ears and poet weeps that the mass has lost its heart too.

Social norms and economic conditions of a particular era play a significant role in shaping, the characteristics and at the same time determining the events of that specific sphere of life, of that part of history. A kind of a historic stimulus, which forms itself out of the agonizing tendencies of the yesterdays, and that which propels the growth for the future, reinforces the present for the likely trajectory of Socialism. The unstinting generosity that shows itself out is not merely the yardstick to the socialist temperament, which often gets itself disguised in the masquerade of a singularity screening, beneath it the pluralistic foundations that originally function, as the edifice of the very concrete structure of its own. Amid the generated intricacies of an era that leaves behind only the glorious nostalgia, of a bygone past and casting on one, the bereavement of the successive losses for which a life time has been spent earnestly for a retrieval Socialism, at least, can be of one like a firefly. Reorganization and synthesis are terms of relevance in the sphere of socialistic discourse, where forces of degeneration and antithesis gain upper hand in the trends of the day, constituted of the 'mesmeric manias'. The underworld enmeshed in the thorns of oppressing forces of degradation, can revive its own vitality and essential spirit of a universal brotherhood, only through the instantaneous installation of a socialist code of conduct, which is viewed as the anti-venom for the venomous spite of the day. It is here , having a forting at this juncture of historic transitions and travesties, one has to seek out a counter- culture that can very subtly be the alter ego of individual as well as 'social persona'. The unacknowledged undercurrents of society and the social constructions with its social contributions in generating a cultural significance have to be brought under close scrutiny for a penetration in the social realities that germinate a social contest leading to socialistic concerns. It is in this context that the poems of Temsula Ao having no compromise with the stark realities of everyday life rendering the pleasurable and the painful, fusing them to correspond to the actualities of day to day life.

The cultural plurality of the Indian social scenario, instigating in the minds of its artisans an unquenchable thirst to be an inveterate democrat adds to the naturalistic, as well as socialistic fervor of each Indian leading him to the path of a socialistic mode of thought process and behavioral strategies. The overarching themes of Socialism, with its diverse dimensions, the multidimensional, multi-perspective, nature of Feminism, benevolence and malevolence of nature and natural phenomenon, the mythical and quasi-mythical figures, range in the poetic world of Temsula Ao. A replica of contemporary social situations replenish the interiors of the largely flexible, textual borders of Temsula Ao, and the vast poetic repertoire allows the poet to rehearse the social norms and traditions and attire them in poetic robes of diction. The menace that even threatens the very existence of one as an individual, having a concrete identity and personality of one's own, having the energy to assert ones 'dependence on oneself, which often ironically termed as independence 'but in reality the supreme mode of slavery, poses before the poet, questions of serious cultural, social and moral conflicts for which she finds herself as the sole hand to write the reply. It is out of this realization that the poems of Temsula Ao germinate:

I hurried past,
Not because I was
Miserly
But that a sudden flash
Streaked through me (*SOMM:17*)

A socialistic pattern of life has a distancing effect from loneliness, which perhaps, may be the one reason why fraternity is very closely allied to the concept Socialism. The agonizing atmosphere, replete with the 'formless fears' of the day, gets further intensified through the fret and fever of loneliness, where the sharper edges of Socialism gradually crumble down, and the concept itself undergoes a process of evaporation. Here a phenomenon of evacuation, from the state of a 'social living' to a state of confinement in one's own 'self living' and that which is not favoured by many, transforms the essential sensibility of an individual. This degradation gets amply exemplified in the poem "Vacuum":

As the last
Handful of dust
Settled on the wood
The earth was healed
Of the gaping wound
But a new wound
Was inflicted.
On a lonely heart
Now filled with
Only ashes and dust. (*SOMM:27*)

The incessant tug of war between the manipulated and the manipulator, often resulting in the downfall of one, especially that of the former and that which constitutes history re-echoes in the poems of Temsula Ao. Humanity sodden with guilt lacks the skill and the will to resort to expiation, a means to sing in the new and sing out the old one. The rivulets of regeneration, many in number and means, gape before one larger consideration, tend to make decisions fluctuate and sometimes even to an outright negation of that. This may, sometimes relegate the attributes of humanity, such as kindness, love, empathy, tenderness etc. and may bring into prominence a sub-culture through the process of a sub-standardization. Temsula Ao, as a poet of greater concern, regarding humanity and human values, has been highly concerned of social value erosion,

Furthermore , dusky social situations, however gloomy it may appear, can have on its borders a tinge of the golden streaks of a mingy Socialism.

Temsula Ao, as one cast into an alien culture of ecstasy, candidly searches even into darkness for brightness and with a firmness of spirit, though undulating at times at the sight of the horrendous hamartia befalling her generation immerses herself with perspicacity, even into the depths of the cacophonous clatter to retrieve the harmony and euphony, because she realizes the extinction of the annoying and the existence of the appealing. She never dissembles the actualities that occur and recur before the dissecting eyes of hers, though, however unpleasant they may seem to be and this is what provided her poetry with the nature of a gusset, contributing to the dissemination of socialist ideas. The gradual deformation of the world into a 'loony-bin', where considerations of many a matter soar high above humanitarian concerns has been instrumented in digging deeper, even to the very roots and foundations of one's origin. Even anatomy has been brought on the dissection table of social respectability and class status where initially physical deformity impedes the path to Socialism and ultimately leads to the total extinction of it. The forced identification of the poet with the lepers, 'where disfigurement is the only nationality' reveals to her many more truths of Socialism than any dogmas could have taught. This painful revelation of a pricking truth, breaking open all the sheaths of sentiments, gushes out in the following lines of "The Valley of the Lepers":

So hastily and fearfully
I withdrew
From the valley
Of those
Condemned to live
With their

Dying
But even today
A certain sunken
Hollow smile
Haunts me wild *(STTTS: 46)*

The atrocities of leprosy, portrayed by Temsula Ao, through which a larger social situation pointed at, that is, how far is Socialism a reality or whether it is a myth and a mania? Amidst the inadequacies and inequalities surging on earth, Temsula Ao is confident to assert establishment of a greater Socialism, depriving one and all of anything and everything. This surreptitious hand of Socialism has been institutionalized in the lives of each individual, irrespective of class, creed distinctions from the very moment of one's birth. The all-encompassing and all-consuming proprietor of Socialism, who, in other words termed as the 'great leveler' has been established by Temsula Ao as the final verdict of Socialism. In the poem "When Death Comes Calling" she speaks:

Does he ring the bell
And show the book
Does he allow you
To get of the hook
Once in a while? *(STT: 26)*

The revitalizing effect of a socialist mode of existence, having the redemptive potential to 'segregate one from seclusion' and thus to integrate diverse and distinct value systems, finds echoes and reechoes in the poetry of Temsula Ao. She lays stress not on diversities, rather on the spirit of Socialism, underlying the diversity. Temsula Ao is a poet, who very successfully infiltrates not merely into one dimension of human life, rather she explores the life generating as well as the life negating forces functioning as undercurrents in the very being of every individual whether he is young or old. An attempt is made by the poet to create a cult of old age, which is far removed from the mainstream life, in the poem "Old" and in turn it voices the sharing of a devastation brought about by time in the form of wrinkles and roughness:

Old age
Is aches and pains
Only loss, no more gains
It is
Lethargy
Of a body
Which once held
Beauty and strength *(STTTS: 24)*

Optimistic outlook in the world, though temporary set back at times hamper the fluidity of life here, keeps the poetry of Temsula Ao a little apart from that of others. She is the one writer, who has a deep rooted faith in the human perseverance and perspicaciously passes judgment on man and humanity at large. She recognizes the power of a social behavior or a gesture and hold, that to be the supreme mode of any kind of boosters, sheltering within its framework the power to lead the humanity away from the crouching dog days lying ahead of them. She speaks of such a worthwhile idea in "The System":

A gentle world,
A tap on the shoulder
And a silent push
Of the mighty pen
Can alter a course
Or see a project through *(STTTS: 43)*

Socialism expounded by Temsula Ao may appear to be mere hogwash, to a cynical eye, but her poetry having a vision and a mission, which is a really noble one, has never been intended to be mere razzmatazz. It addresses the individual, the society and the world, with the mission of redressing its pangs through which every one can dream of a path of red-carpet into the future. While living in an era of indifference and interferences, both of which of course, suicidal, Temsula Ao's poetry serves the function of a pointer in the wintry landscape of modern existence. Amidst the resplendent charm of the lines and their musicality, one is able to retrace a tinge of a melancholic fervor, generated mostly from a realization of the crumbling edifices of modern living. Temsula Ao, as a writer, takes special care to keep her writing away from sliding down into a state of prolixity which certainly has become a feature of the present day literature. As an artist engaged in the process of artistry and beautification, Temsula Ao keeps herself close to the heart of the society, where she can hear even the dry pulse of a throbbing heart of Socialism that stands in the verge of extinction. But the future oriented philosophy of her, propels her into the future, where certainly one could see the glimmer of hope which may resemble that of the fertile golden bygone past. Thus Temsula Ao as a missionary and a visionary keeps in the private fantasies, as the most cherished one, a dream of a euphoric socialist society.

2. Feminism in the Poetry of Temsula Ao

There are not many writers in the North-East of India who have dealt with issues, concerning woman as Temsula Ao has. Her empathy, love and concern for the woman are explicitly reflected in her poem "Woman". Initially she seems to have accepted the plight of woman, in the contemporary society:

> Nature fashioned her thus
> To bear the burden
> To hold the seed
> And feed
> Every other need
> But hers. (*STT:* 22)

The use of alliteration in the last part is praiseworthy. Has nature really fashioned woman to bear the entire burden on her own shoulders? Is she to accept male chauvinism, and crawl under the feet of man forever? The poet takes an unpredictable turn when she says:

But woman
Thus fashioned
Thus oppressed
Beguiled and betrayed,
Sometimes rebelled
To break the mould
And shake of the hold
That nature devised
and man improvised. (*STT*: 22)

The poet is one among the few who rebels to break the mould, and shake off the "hold" that nature devised and man improvised. Woman is fashioned, as per the will of man and thus she is oppressed, beguiled and betrayed. Now she has realized that the only way to break away from the oppressors is to rebel tooth and nail. There are a number of feminists leading this struggle, the poet being one of them cannot but do her bit by doing justice to herself in her poems. The dichotomy between the 'subject' and the 'other'- that is viewed as the negative 'object'- which has been created for the establishment and the perpetration of the dominance of men and the subordination of the women, had a diaphanous purpose hidden beneath it. The dictated norms of the patriarchal society, often hindering the path of woman to self realization, nipped the bud of the productive and creative potentials of the womenfolk. The cultural economic, social and even moral pervasions seen with contempt , on the peripheral platform but acknowledged and appreciated at root, enigmatic sphere, were even, attributed to the woman, seen as the 'frail creature'. Acquiescence and timidity were nailed on women along with the emotional fluctuations seen by the male as the root cause of frailty, for the purpose of a confinement to make the female subordinate, complementary and submissive to the masculine desires and enterprises.

Temsula Ao, a sharer of the feminine psyche and sensibility and having the feminine residual current flowing through the inner layers of the psyche, poses before the patriarchal society though the depicting of the crushed and withered feminine spirit, a series of sorrow stricken queries regarding the infallibility of the masculine gender - biased value systems that seem to be pontificating all about the sensations and sensibilities of a woman. 'Don't's become the oft repeated terms, when compared to the 'do's' in the social and familial existence of a woman. In "The Creator" Temsula Ao portrays the essential sorrow of a woman experienced in the stampede in the modern life in a male-oriented, male-governed world. Here the imprisoned self of a woman gets unveiled:

But burdened
With the woman in me
The catcher
Became the caught
Struggling to preserve
The selve from desolving
Into a domestic web
And from becoming
The nameless half
Of the entire man *(SOMM: 12)*

Even while undergoing the traumas of womanhood Temsula Ao does not stand as an advocate of female gullibility, rather woman is made an institution in herself and then raises her above even the male, through the ornamentation of an aura of motherhood. The transformatory role, an expedition from womanhood to the ever glorious motherhood, gets explicated in the following role and it becomes an assertion, not merely of womanhood but of the strength and dynamism of a woman:

I am a woman
And a woman creates
Therefore
I shall create
The real me
And a brave new world *(SOMM: 13)*

The capacity for endurance of a woman, amidst the turbulences of day to day life is a recurrent theme in Temsula Ao, and often her role is that of the observer as she who stands as silent witness and also the recipient of the degeneracy. All the diverse roles played by the woman in the social context- that of a mother, daughter, sister etc. often becomes a pointing finger at the idiosyncrasies of the society but even then her mighty wings of integrity are there as a shelter to her kith and kin. Temsula Ao, very powerfully strikes at the cancerous selfishness and hostility, existing in man-woman or rather husband-wife, relationship that eats away at their genuinity and humanity, their strength and their integrity. She explicates how the internalized values without proper realization of the physical, spiritual and emotional needs of the counterpart germinate a kind of monstrosity of vacuum in relationships. The poem "Combat" adequately envisages this aspect; where even the mesmeric conjugal bliss, gets itself redefined as a kind of a combat and this poem certainly delves deeper into a contemporary social reality:

An unnamed combat
Persisted all through
The endless night
When body touched body
But failed to ignite *(SOMM: 57)*

The demonic projections of men's libidinous desire asserting itself in the form of masculine power, The woman on the other hand, with fantastic dreams centred on their little world, comprising of the beloved ones of the household, realize in the flux of time, the tragic dimension attached to their aspiration and how easily they crumble down to 'nothingness'. This context of man-woman relationship is one of the predator-prey relationships, where man, with his head erect, places himself on the high pedestal of the winner and under him the dare faced reality, -the woman- assumes the position of a diminutive i.e. the looser. Their shattered dreams fall on them like an avalanche, magnificent in the zenith and nothing more than little pieces of ice once fallen, reiterating the presence of unsympathetic shackles of traditions and customs that bind them even from being simple dreamers. The poem "Pawned" speaks of such a miserable situation:

But when I went back to him
With riches
To redeem my dream

He said-
there can be no redemption
For a dream once pawned
Is a dream for ever gone *(STTTS: 36)*

Temsula Ao, the best and truest historian of the woman's region, has been the vital 'conscience' of the woman's psyche and in her we can find an aching sensibility to the confusions and lose of values of the era, especially the maltreatment meted out to woman whose life has been largely viewed as a part of a sub-culture. There is a kind of striking similarity between the philosophy of Temsula Ao and that of William Faulkner, the most original and assimilating writer of the American literary world. Both these writers have great faith in man, declining to accept the end of man and believing that man will not merely endure but he will prevail. Providing it a final glow with the attribution of a feminine spirit, Temsula Ao reserves her deepest pity for the isolated, the poor, the oppressed, the down trodden, the frustrated, the frightened and above all for women in lonely conflict against the forces of existence and destiny.

The poem "Requiem" illustrates a really disturbing situation, which became instrumental in consuming the lives of many a woman in the flames of avarice. Thus having reserved the sympathy for the underdogs-women-she portrays a compelling picture of the radical imperfection in the society's 'personality', which is the cause root of its tragedy and glory. The poet asks:

Who will mourn?
Who will mourn this blackened mass?
The charred
Of a recent blushing bride
Roasted on the pyre
Of avarice...... *(STT: 43)*

Temsula Ao manipulates the Indian historiography in such a way as to erase the mythical aura which had blighted it, and to form powerful, new mythic images, often unpleasant and painful to lead to knowledge. According to Temsula Ao, each woman experiences, an experience of the waste-lender and the world in which they dwell is one, where there is sin without any hope of redemption, struggle without the possibility of victory, suffering without meaning or purpose, sex without love and love without fulfillment. This discretion or bareness, undergone by women is fused with the bareness of the earth, and this is what makes her lament for the earth, which, in a way, is a sorrow-stricken cry for women. In "Lament for Earth" she says:

Grieve for the —— of an earth

That was once —— vibrant
Virgin *(STS: 47)*

Beneath the technical virtuosity of the poems, beneath the portrait of the decaying and degenerating self of womanhood and the emergence of the modern patriarchal order, the real theme of Temsula Ao's poetry is basically the disenchantment of an evil maturity that lies at the root level of the problems. This is what enhances the distortions and dilemmas, as portrayed in the life of a tree in "An old Tree" eating away at the personality of a woman:

Thus I stand now
Ungainly and unsure
Of I shall endure
This winter's frost
Or next summer's rains" *(SOMM: 36)*

Each woman experiences a kind of a perpetual winter without a progressive hope for a spring, like Shelley, in their social life. They are afraid of the winter's frost and the summer's rains, both having the potential to bestow tremor in these frail beings having already received a series of devastating experiences and are at the verge of an extinction. The poem "Everest" attempts a microscopic analysis though a hidden one, of the all dwarfing majesty of the male. Even those glorious ones are destined to be submissive 'microbes' there under the magnificence of the outstretched arms of him. The poem, "With an Element of Irony" opens up:

In the misty horizon
He sits majestic
Dwarfing
All the giants around him
With a presence
That is only his *(SOMM: 41)*

The small/big dichotomy plays a very suggestive role in the poems of Temsula Ao, just as in the celebrated work *The God of Small Things (1997)* by Arundhati Roy. The small is always destined to be the victims, the sufferer, the loser and above all the icon of failure, whereas the big assumes a colonial figure over the small with all authority and unlimited power and thus, become the exploiter and the winner. Women have been destined to play the role of the small and above their broods the big to hatch the inevitable disaster. The life of the small has always been defined in terms of the 'Mombatti' which can produce only a slander flame and which is exposed to the turbulent winds at the risk of extinction at any moment.

Every woman's life, in the contemporary society, becomes a saga of suffering and torture. The agonies and afflictions of a single, helpless woman in an extremely hostile world becomes one of the thematic concerns of the poetry of Temsula Ao in "Moon-Rise." The poet redraws the portrait of a woman in modern, consumerist society, though the depiction of a lonely moon:

Thus she stands,
Steeped of her romance
Bereft of her enchantment
And dissolves
Into unwilling oblivion
Until
The next moon-rise *(STTTS: 20)*

The desolation and isolation experienced by woman, amidst the hallabaloos of the day, find apt representation here. The complex dynamics of the patriarchal social setup has assigned a definite role for women as a passive, submissive, all enduring one where womanhood is very largely defined on the basis of motherhood. All these patriarchal prejudices get dismantled in the hands of Temsula Ao. The multiple layers of tragedy, of the unpleasant and unlucky existence created by religious taboos and social morality in the life of a woman gets questioned by Temsula Ao. Her poetry lays bare before the reader a world that is rotten, and voices of emotions receive scant attention. Thus Temsula Ao, through her poetry represents the excruciating agony experienced by women and at the same time establishes in concrete form the spirit of the feminine and the identity of womenfolk. The inescapable plight into which each woman is cast, where she carries the burden of anxieties, at the realization of motherhood, makes a relation impossible and this mortified self of a woman screaming aloud to the entire generation, is visible in the poem "The Serpent and I":

> Leaving me
> Mortified
> Matriarch
> To a fallen race
> Beguild into knowledge
> Hid from the distant Gods *(STS: 53)*

Temsula Ao makes poetry a medium through which the shed of golden feathers of the past and the resultant agony, especially of women, are portrayed, with full vigour and vitality. The poet's ability to convert complex and abstract thoughts, into concrete and simple forms is passion, in the world of human affairs. Everyday life is considered to be a climb to the top of the mountain, which each individual does. The poet does not consider life as a bed of roses. However difficult life is, the poet opines:

> An inner passion builds,
> An urge begins to thrill
> To the challenge
> Of the mountain,
> With its secret
> And its majesty. (*STTT:* 12)

Thus, the poet is of the view that life is to be lived. Nothing in life is to be feared, everything is just to be understood. All the sorrows and pains that one undergoes is a part of it. Seeing from a distance, one would feel that life has hidden a lot of secrets in it like a mountain. On reaching the top of the mountain, the mountaineer becomes aware of the loftiness in the sky, and an expanse in the horizon beyond the reach of the highest mountain. The poet clearly points out that anyone who has lived and failed, in finding the secrets of life have lived in vain. Life, when seen from a distance seems:

> The mountain stands,
> Impassive, challenging,
> Imposing, dominating,
> Reposing, secretive
> And smugly benign. (*STTTS:* 12)

The poet looks at life as a whole which has all the qualities mentioned in the above mentioned stanza. For the purpose of the present study, let us analyze the social significance of the poem, especially in relation to 'normal life' in North-East India. Repeated terror attacks in the region have made life a horrible experience for the common man. That is why the poet sings:

> You go through pain,
> You go through peril,
> And finally gain
> The top of the mountain. (*STTTS:* 12)

A sense of passive acceptance of the edifice and the hardships that comes out of it prevails in the poem. The poet wants the readers to detach themselves from their 'lives' and look at life as a separate whole. She believes that only then one would be able to reject the illusion, that life is all joy and happiness. While analyzing oneself after reaching the top of the mountain one may realize that it was just nothing, yet everyone has to travel the distance from the plains to the mountain, from birth to death.

The poem entitled "To the Children of the World" is not intended to regale the readers, but to make them ponder. The poem deals with some of the pivotal issues, that de facto occur in the minds of everyone no matter how least interested they are in the philosophy of life. The poem opens with an advice:

> To all you children who are born,
> And are yet to be born,
> Just one word of advice -
> Never ask
> Why you were born. (*STTTS:* 19)

The poet is nct afraid of the question but she already has the answer to this question: Life carries no specific purpose, and it is just a mystery which is completely beyond anyone's ken. The poem is written in blank verse, and has just twenty three lines which provoke the reader to think. The society gives no reason as to why some of us are born poor and some rich. Philosophical questioning would not help us arrive at a conclusion. The poem reiterates the famous saying of George Orwell. In his book *Animal Farm (2005)* he says, 'all animals are equals, but some animals are more equal than other animals.' *(Orwell .2005: 114).* Here, it needs to be emphasized that Temsula Ao's poetry is not mere frivolous jugglery of words and porno stuff, but very serious attempts to answer philosophical and sociological questions. The poem showcases the plight of the poor women not only in our country but anywhere in the world. Women are sexually abused by their employers, superiors, colleagues, and some of us are simply the result of this sort of exploitation. The poetess also raises her voice against social inequality in this poem. The cynosure of all eyes in this poem would be the second stanza, which has employed no figure of speech or any other such poetic device:

Some of you were born
To inherit
The plunder of the ages
And some-
Because the midwife's portion
Was not strong enough.
But no one
Will tell you this
So never ask
Why you were born. (*STTTS:* 19)

Some of the poems of Temsula Ao have a mesmerizing impact on the readers. The best example for this may be the poem, "When Death Comes Calling" from the collection *Songs That Tell*. The poem commands significance on account of the theme it deals with. Man's progress in the field of science and technology and the ability to extent the span of human life is appreciated in the poem. She reminds the readers the fact that man has not defeated death and is still a prey to death, which comes at unexpected hours wearing a mask. The poem has its social significance too because she warns the readers of the possibility of the arrival of death at any moment, expected or unexpected. The poet asks some of the very striking questions:

When death comes calling now a days
Does he wear a mask
Or does he display an identity card
Printed in gold and edged with black?
Does he ride his jet
Fly on his wings
Or simply walk. (*STT:* 26)

The poem "When death comes calling" treats a metaphysical issue. The poem is an intelligent attempt in the direction of self-realization, though it affects metaphysics.

3. Conclusion

Temsula Ao's poems, are an expression of the poet's companionship with recollections and thereby a remedy. Amrit Joyti Mahanta rightly comments,

To Temsula's credit, she succeeds in maintaining a distance from subscribing to any particular set of opinion while bringing forth the pain and suffering of the North-East people as a community and shaking the readers' conscience *(2006: Online ed).*

Though the Man is born alone, lives alone and dies alone, yet the thought of loneliness is a far-fetched notion. Reminiscing the past, the present leaves no time for loneliness, but adds mental strength and goodwill inspirations. Temsula Ao presents her eco-feminist-humanist-sermons in her songs. A blithe singer of lyrical ballads, she is a dreamer of an ecofriendly environment in the progress of the nation. The poet believes, that women can in principle, undertake any activity- political, and intellectual, as well as a man can, and thus one should not discriminate against women in virtue of their womanhood. The feminist in Temsula Ao becomes a social force.

In a country where its entire population is governed by creed and greed, religion and region Temsula Ao's poetry stands apart. She is obviously hurt when things go wrong and reflect a wounded heart in some of the poems. Her poetry records hard truth in all their colors. The very titles of her collections reveal an inexplicable attempt to be understood but not to be accepted. Her aim is 'to tell' or at least to 'try to say' to a people that seldom listen to any other creed than theirs. Her poetry reiterates that the strategy of love is still relevant and powerful in the battlefield of hate no matter what medium one uses to convey it.

Temsula Ao is a poet of the battered and the marginalized-a poet who sings because she cannot stop singing of the untold miseries and of a great culture. Temsula Ao's poems are a reckoning of the philosophy of Socialism and the strength of Feminism, as she threads gently upon nature and society. As a silent poet of variety Temsula Ao, may be rightly called "The Nightingale of North-Eastern India." *(Das:* proceedings of NEIFES, *Vol 3. p. 26)* One can soothingly assume that her poetry, keeps the wrinkles out of the mind and spirit.

4

Romance of Socialism and Feminism in the Poetic Works of Monalisa Changkija

1. Socialism in Monalisa Changkija's Poetry

Monalisa Changkija can be called, as a great cartographer of ordinary lives. Most of her poems deal with the themes of Socialism and Feminism. She is gifted with a journalist's eye, and poetess' gift for metaphor. Romance and politics, sensuous lyricism and fiery passion mingle inextricably in her poetry. One of the most distinguishable characteristics of her poetry is her sympathy with the oppressed. Despite interesting insights and images, the reader's movement within the poetry is confined. She has a gift for images, and simplicity, of expression. Her poetry shows her talent for drawing inspiration from the horrible social background, in which she lives. A variety of themes, styles and moods are interwoven to attain not only pleasure, but a change in the lives of the readers. The poet has to her credit two volumes of poetry:

1. *Weapons of Words on Pages of Pain* (1993)
2. *Monsoon Mourning (2007)*

Articulation underwent unprecedented aberration, through the superabundance of silence that cast a spell of frigidity in human life, in the 21st century. The flavour and aroma of a concrete identity that gets defined on the social, economical, cultural and spiritual spheres, take a departure from their originality. The irredeemable illness of estrangement and enslavement, brought about mainly through the 'silence' of the day, projects itself out as a harbinger of the decline of human values and the dramatic downfall of the human race, from the dignified pedestal. Prophesies of the past, regarding the future, drew before the eye span of one a callous picture, entwined in domestic and global violence. On the fringes of an assumed social security, one comes to encounter, not through an arduous task of "internal interference", the hazardous forces crouching with the potential for extinction. This mundane reality, once overlooked, may demand a larger payment especially from a social group constituted of individuals of 'uniqueness and diversity', which may pave the way for a lopsided situation in all the dimensions of social being.

'Democratic decadence' a terminology that assumed currency in the wake of the 21st century, characterized by trendy ideals and simulated social doctrines, and which perpetrated social injustice, subsequently formulated a social situation of individual as well as moral decadence. The rapacious tendencies, born out as the off-springs of the life negating forces of modernity, on the one hand, glamourizes the lives of a few who are "more equal', and on the other hand, pushes down the majority, who are 'not even equal' into the deepest recesses of a worm like existence; camouflaging the extent of misery experienced by this marginalized underdogs of the day. The reincarnation of social values which is part of a larger nexus of value systems, to be made possible, requires the harmonious blending of thought and action. But often a deviation from the expected aim, though an unintentional one, lead to a greater discord resulting in a kerfuffle, where the expected margin of achievement gradually transforms into the unexpected boundary of unattainment.

Socialism while being a mirage in the everyday actualities

of the day, still has the power of a gavel that can attract many an eyes and ears to a specific point of the need of a flexible social being. The dejection experienced by many through the rejection of "many" – a really agonizing phenomenon- opens before a sensitive mind cascades of questions regarding Socialism. It is here, Monalisa Changkija, like a supernova, rises above other writers, with her preoccupation with the socialist concerns, which are not merely peripheral, rather they manifest a deep rooted anguish over the hither to neglected concept of a socialist welfare state. Rejuvenation, a key term in the critical discussions of modern social scenario, has become the demand of the day, as the flickering slender flames of Socialism encounter the threat of extinction from the oppressive forces arising from many corners in many forms. In every nook and corner of contemporary life, symptoms of socio- cultural vandalisms appear assuming the forms of degenerative forces and executing the functions of a manipulator of demolitions. Even though forces of generativity, imbued with the power to alter the social situations and the hard biting realities akin to it, are deployed to counter the devastative tendencies; often what is bequeathed to the generations to come is nothing, but the multiplicity of troubles born out of these diffused forces. As far as Monalisa Changkija is concerned, it is not a dilettante approach that she attempts towards these social issues; rather, while piercing through the prismatic harshness of social realities, she leaves behind a rich legacy of conclusions, through which a greater consolation to the brittle creatures of the society.

Amidst the nightmarish occurrences of the world, where life gets defined largely on the basis of power politics and monetary status, Monalisa Changkija accumulates courage and determination negotiate with the oppressive forces for a common brotherhood, which, to her is the zenith of Socialism. The poet's stand reminds mankind of what Joan of Arc declared,

I am not afraid. I am born to do this. *(Davies.2006: 26)*

Monalisa Changkija is aware of the stark reality that the oppressors take their face of pleasure on earth by making the life of the marginalized bitter and black with sorrow, though the force exerted on them to consume even the sediment of segregation. The neurotic gluttony, of the day, of course for material growth, riles Changkija, but from the perspective of a poet she makes a shakedown into the formative role, especially of a great assertion, played by such social realities and thus she, with Hemingway, makes a thunderous assertion –'one can be destroyed, but cannot be defeated.' In the poem "Shoot":

> Shoot I give you my word, we will not move
> Shoot, you, all of you who have us covered from your sides
> You have us now the way you want, so shoot
> Shoot and claim victory it's all yours
> We will stand firm and not move
> From our dreams of brotherhood *(MM: 35)*

Here, Monalisa Changkija, affirms the staunch support, required by and provided to a group of people, who to the eyes of the well to do members of the society, who are the beneficiaries of the comforts of the society and at the same time cannibalize the menial and meager of the poor, for their intensified joys may appear to be mere ugly scraggy stereotypes, devoid of any attributes of an individual. Her poetry becomes a cannonade of words pregnant with emotions, especially due to the agony caused by the sorry situation of the society. The metallic framework of the society that is instrumental in the formation of the 'upper' and the lower or the 'victimizer and the victimized' undergoes a restructuring process in the hands of Monalisa Changkija.

Monalisa's poetry is the art of serious efforts, daring intrinsic layers, and the pleasurable experiences. Her style is persuasive, her thoughts simple, and yet intellectual, aimed at expressing falling values in society. Her poetry is outstanding, and can be interpreted in multiple ways. She is a realist portraying social upheavals. At the same time, one should remember that Monalisa's poetry is not a mere cadenced ululation. She often resorts to downright condemnation of such social upsets. It is not the job of the poets to take sides. Yet Monalisa sides the battered section of the society. She is a socialist par excellence, as far as the poets from the North-East are concerned. Monalisa Changkija writes in a time of terror. The reader feels that poetry comes out better when dealing with terror. She depicts atrocities and more so, the atmosphere of terror. Her poetry often responds to the malfunctioning political system with defiance, and great courage. This irresistibility to portray social upsets is one of the prominent characteristics of Monalisa Changkija's poetry. It seems as if violence is let loose in the North-East by the divine hand. Death, violence and bloodshed occupy the entire space in the front pages of the newspapers of the North-East. The poet does not hesitate to bow before those who will not listen. Her love for society has gained priority over anything else for she prays:

> Stop this night mare, I pray
> Wherein my people, victims of
> Geography, history and politics
> Have become prized booty
> To be over powered and possessed
> By those who will not listen (*MM:* 34)

She knows full well that her pleadings fall over deaf ears. But her love, the love for those battered does not let her keep silence. She is conscious politically, socially, historically and in many more ways. She is no doubt a realist who understands things as they are. She does not live in a dream world, but hopes and prayers that her dreams may come true. She is not a coward to crawl under the feet of the oppressors. In the poem "Shoot" an angry, down to earth realist Monalisa Changkija braves:

Go ahead, shoot and blast us to eternity
I give you my word, we will not move
Neither from our stand nor to distract your aim
Shoot, what's stopping you?
What's making you tremble?
Shoot I give you my word, we will not move
Shoot, you, all of you who have us covered from your sides
You have us now the way you want, so shoot. (*MM:* 35)

The repetition of the word 'shoot' trembles the reader. It is not only an angry expression of the social realities, but here the poet reveals who the real cowards are, when she wrote; "You have us now the way you want, so shoot." Monalisa never misses her aim. Each word is carefully selected and thoughtfully arranged, that they hit the goal no matter how far it is. Even the least interested reader understands, her target which is as fixed as a door nail:

Surely you are confident of world opinion
Surely you are convinced you are right
So shoot, i give you my word, we will not move
Shoot, after all we are only an inconvenience of a few lakh souls (*MM:* 35)

The elements of Socialism found in Monalisa's poetry cannot be questioned. No doubt, she is the poet socially conscious and committed. Her clear eyed gaze uncovers the politics of gender. Her love and sympathy for the second sex and the poor are reflected in almost all her poems. The most notable characteristic of her poetry is the harsh reality that is entwined. She blows in as a robust, energetic breath of fresh air taking the readers along with her and making them feel the more painful side of life. Death, however tragic it may be and often attributed with majesty and grandeur under the term 'sacrifice' if it's for a noble and novel cause, is redefined by the poet and the aim is not the glorification of death or the dead rather death, here paradoxically becomes 'life'. In other words for Monalisa Changkija, death, once embraced for establishing a socialist order of life, becomes synonymous with life. Here each mutilation received on the body, bridges the gap between the myth of Socialism and the reality of Socialism and then each wound on the physique provides flesh and blood to a socialist order and thus the absence of breath in a human body indicates the presence of breath – i.e. life – in the lives of many. The poem "Not Be Dead" amply illustrates this:

If Tomorrow
My body
Is riddled
With bullets,
I shall not be dead
Nor will I
Be defeated and silenced *(MM: 21)*

Certainly, this poem exemplifies not a halcyon life, blessed in everything rather it aims at the elevation of a mode of life, certainly afflicted by the agony of leading it forward, and which is one of greater endurance, that has been viewed by the 'Blessed Beings' of the society as a gimcrack existence. Even this tattered body, by the shower of bullets has a tale of Socialism to tell as this suffering is not a mere gimmick, but a sacrifice for a true cause. The dissolution of personal dreams and self-centered ego- centric aspirations until it gives way for a collective dream of a progressive society, should be the pedestal on which the socialist structure has to be built on. The cantankerous tendencies, usually born out of the misplacement of ideas and ideologies in the social group or a social context can submerge one in a whirlpool of hatred, leading society to a shambolic, fancy state. But once queries are made to a fellow being in the society about his needs, requirements and expectations, not with a purpose just to know them, but with an intention to assist them, it can lead to the evolution of Socialism through a feeling of oneness characterized by mutual sharing and caring. The moment one plays a nocturne to celebrate the victory of another and shed a teardrop at the sight of a woebegone person, a symbol of participation, a rare Socialism is born and a society where people of such charismatic fervor live can be called a paragon of Socialism. Monalisa Changkija openly declines the life of the 'islanders' and advocates a handy Socialism in "Just so You Know that":

> Yes, I have grieved at your losses
> Personal and professional
> And celebrated your triumphs
> As if they were mine,
> Though I may seen uncaring
> Because I am never around
> To hold your hands *(WoWoPoP: 44)*

Monalisa Changkija unlike other writers never makes use of poetry as a peg to hang her personal philosophy, on the contrary she suavely, without much ornamentation speaks of the 'subaltern' - the poor, marginalized and socially neglected and oppressed. Even while being conscious of the zing in human personality to perform the hitherto unperformed and alter the unaltered and thus to trespass into the world of enigmas, there lingers an element of trepidation listening to the squeal of the horrible and horrifying anguish of humanity brought about largely by the shackles with which he is bound. Monalisa Changkija, like a polemicist, lays bare before the very eyes of the reader, who often far removed from reality by way of the disguises of the world, the antithesis of human beings in their potential level. The foolhardiness, often mistaken for valiance, deprives one of farther chances of the attainment of Socialism and the risible endeavours made to redraw the once charted course of action for the attainment of the Eden in their life, finally make them frustrated beings. This sharp contrast between the glorious expectations and the eerie actualities, mostly culminating in frustration is drawn in bright colours in "Dare I call you Friend?" Here the predator becomes the prey and here we pay witness to an inchoate and ironic Socialism:

Ah, but we humans
Are capable of much beyond our dreams
Of donning facades
There by chaining ourselves to live sentences
And feeling smug
Over our cleverness *(WoWoPoP: 41)*

The flabby social life of the day, which for the majority, is really nightmarish due to the socio-political uprisings, and a ritzy one for a minority, once pierced deeper into its core, opens before the poet's eyes the scope for a luminous future. The sluggishness of modern social life, expressing a winter with all its smog and snow fall, repudiates the advent of a spring. But Monalisa Changkija, like Shelley, is optimistic of the reincarnation of a blooming spring out of the ashes of the present day devastations and this phoenix like resurrection will be one for the reconstruction of a socialist mode of life, which has been preordained by the life style of the forefathers - Monalisa Changkija is hopeful that the claptrap and clamour of the present day, which echoes with the distress of humanity will ultimately blend into a euphony vibrating with all enthusiasm as if in a cadenza. This optimistic outlook, though tinged with sorrow for a series of losses that have been experienced by a generation in the course of history, opens up before the reader in "One of These Decades":

One of these decades when our dreams
Become as real as the nightmare how

We will gather around the fire
On moonlit nights, as did our forefathers
And silence the gunfire with our songs
Loud and clear across our green hills
In rhythm with all humanity
To keep our date with destiny *(MM: 10)*

Monalisa Changkija attempts a critique of violence which is inherent in personal as well as social relationship. The grandiloquence, with which the theme of violence has been depicted by many in literature, undergoes a purging effect, when Monalisa Changkija defines violence in crystal clear terms, as a real blockade in the attainment of a socialist pattern of society. She attempts not a definition of violence, rather a search into the cause of violence and finds its roots in the hopeless and helpless plight of man and thus makes one aware that the eradication of violence, for social progress, can be done only through a change in social patterns and situations; she says:

Man's inadequacies
And insecurity
Speak in the
Language of violence *(WoWoPoP: 4)*

The horrible and horrifying, assuming the forms violence and tragedies and depriving one of a peaceful existence merge into the lives of the people to generate a vast plethora of disequilibrium thereby shaking the very foundations of Socialism. Under the wide-spread wings of terror, where an individual fails to find consolation, there are a few, expectantly, with uplifted faces, waiting for a homely, socialist life. Though peace, in the near future, is a chimerical fascination or an illusion, never do they falter from their dreams of Socialism and Monalisa's poetry - a means of expression of exasperations-become icons of such un assuaging determination. They are like pampered children brought up under blindfolded parents, and whose mischief is never seen and who like Kazantzakis' Zorba even celebrate failures and defeats with a few rollicking steps, challenging even the incantations of old age and death. In the poem "Child of Cain", Monalisa Changkija makes the contours of the magical spell of life and the minatory presence of death submerge, where choices are left open before an individual. Here too, she opens up doors, to flexible Socialism; and an instance of death even culminates in the inception of a kind of Socialism which is part of a collective response. The poem concludes with the following lines:

> Some of us consider life too precious
> To live it under the shadow of fear
> Or under any shadow
> Call us foolish, call us anything
> Because no words can describe
> Our zest for life
> Or our contempt of death *(MM: 24)*

Obligation has a seductive appearance in the poetic world of Monalisa Changkija, as she considers poetry not a mere sedentary work done at leisure hours, rather as part of the trenchantly expressed realities and viewpoints. She, like a woodpecker, searches deep into the thin walls of social realities, to find out the withered, wishy-washy Socialism, suffocating in the modern life of 'empirical extravaganza' and makes a strenuous attempt to revivify it by reminding one of obligations, through which she believes, Socialism can be reestablished on earth. The tremor inflicted on Socialism by a sequence of forces which if not hindered, would articulate only disaster to the conservatory of Socialism. Duty-bound generations who have a consensus on the establishment of a socialist pattern of life and who never connive to any destructive proposals have to be germinated out of the melee to bring Socialism a reality. The mellifluous tone of any philosophy, without conscientiousness regarding over obligations will ever make Socialism a mirage beyond the grasp of one, resulting in perpetual lament over what is gone beyond and beneath retrieval. This self same idea, with an assertion of the scorching social situation and the need for a reawakening into ones obligations is presented in *Monsoon Mourning*. The opening poem in the collection titled *Monsoon Mourning*:

I searched for sanity
In the sophisticated sapience
Of savants from lands
Extrinsic to my conscience
Forgetting my sympathies
Suppressing my sensitivities
Disowning my responsibilities
To the hunger and thirst of
My blood brothers
Who need my hands
In their hour
Of our desperation *(MM: 3)*

The second part of the collection, *Weapons of Words on Pages of Pain* is largely social in nature. The poem entitled "Not Be Dead" is penned, keeping the journalist community of Nagaland in mind. The poem is especially dedicated to Chalie Kevichusa, Editor of *Ura Mail* who fell prey to assassins' bullets. The poem glorifies the immortality of the written words, and the power it has to change the human lives. People who use terror as a means to realize their selfish goals, fail to encompass the fact their bullets can only kill the physical self of the writer. They cannot defeat the poets; neither can they prevent him/her from influencing the people. The poem hails those that are destructed in the process of instruction. The poem is didactic just like any other poem, by the poet. The poem is not a masquerade of any sort:

If tomorrow
My body
Is riddled
With bullets,
I shall not be dead. (*MM:* 21)

Such an event would only mean the capitulation of people who cannot think beyond the AK-47. They are hired by people who are afraid to face reality as it is. But writers are different, they are not afraid to speak the truth, no matter what the outcome is.

The second collection of poetry by Monalisa Changkija *Monsoon Mourning* is an excellent piece of 'serious effort' which exhumes the potential of 'the writing art'. Looking at poetry in an uncanny way, she addresses issues which are core to every human heart in a refreshing and innovative style. Her daring inter-textual layers, both overt and covert with simple intellectual thoughts, indicate that Monalisa is a champion of issues pertaining to the society.

The poem entitled "If Only" showcases the attitude of an average person, who is afraid to come out from the comfort zone. People do not open their minds for fear of revealing their real self. The poet brings the cat out of the bag:

It's not reprisals and retributions I fear.
But I hold my peace
For you cannot think and look beyond
The space you've imprisoned yourself
Into. (*MM:* 16)

One of the most striking poems included in this collection is "Cain's Shoes". The poet has adopted a different approach; the poem treats a social issue in a personal manner. The poet criticizes people who stand aside and murmur what ought to be:

It's easy, much too easy to opine,
aver and assert
what ought to be. (*MM:* 22)

This poem takes us into the deeper realities of everyday life. Man has a bit of goodness and vice in him, that is inborn. Using current events and persons still alive, the poet unveils the fact that people always find reasons for what they do. We have the innate tendency to justify our thoughts and actions:

Talk to George Bush Junior
Or Osama Bin Laden;
They will tell you,
They find themselves
In Cain's shoes today. (*MM:* 22)

The poem reveals a terrifying fact that things are moving out of our control. We look at the horrifying realities of the world from a distance and so things hardly ever resemble reality. We fail to see the bleeding and moaning ground. The poem is refining in character. The poem gives ample opportunities for the readers' movement within it despite interesting insights and images.

Thus the poetry of Monalisa Changkija croons, with all vigour to instill and ignite the mind cherishing Socialism, to act against the degenerative forces and to harvest the mellow Socialism, where existence is not synonymous with extinction rather it echoes with the rhythms of co-existence and co-operation. This is the sense, spirit and savor of her poetry, uplifting Socialism above the smokescreens of hypocrisy. The poetry of Monalisa Changkija, echo the reflections of Dr. S. Radhakrishnan,

> If our mind is peaceful and loving, peace and bliss will follow us. If it be hateful and aggressive, trouble and distress will cloud our path. Grief and

> disaster will come out of ill-will; health and order will come out of goodwill. Let us break with sterile thoughts of the past and break new grounds."

In the collection *Weapons of Words on Pages of Pain*, the poet shares her thoughts and feelings on matters, both personal and political. The second part of the collection, *Words of Miscellany* is personal in nature. Most of the poems in this part are manifestations, of the reflection of the poet, of those people who have colored, her past and are continuing to color her present. This part also reflects the lives of individuals in the social set-up. She knows it does, for they are realities in every society and her society is no exception. Since the stratification of women affects a large session of the society she calls it political. For the very reason let us call it social too.

Twenty years of life as a journalist has made the poet realize, the need to stand firm on one's convictions for the future of the society which is dearly loved. That is the reason why her poetry is very disturbing.

2. Feminism in the Poetry of Monalisa Changkija

The first part of the collection of *Weapons of Words on Pages of Pain,* reflects the poet's thoughts on battered and abused women, on domestic violence and on women's ability to rise above the "second class citizenry". The poet's quest to search for Women's identity in a highly patriarchal society unveils itself in many of the poems. The poet has no doubt as to whether the marginalization of women exists in the society.

For the purpose of the present study, we shall begin with the first part of this collection, which is an in- depth of how Monalisa Changkija view women, vis-à-vis the world. It also tries to analyze how the world sees women. The female identity, often unacknowledged by the male doctrines , and which often creates an emotional hiatus between the male and the female, whatever be the sort of relationship existing- whether husband- wife, father-daughter, mother-son or brother- sister- comprises within it a kind of a sentimentally diluted charm.The outrageous reactions meted out to a woman by patriarchy and the conclaves attended by his psyche along with the collective male psyche in order to come up with the ways and devices with which impositions are to be made on the feminine spirit, generate pain, anguish, isolation and even emotional deprivation in a female, evaluated from a wider perspective, this pathetic plight of women frame a legend, one of misery and showering fears. The yelping of a woman, heard only when it exceeds the barriers of tortures, has been made to subside by the patriarchy for the flowering and fruition of the patriarchal norms. The vested interests of the male dominated society, often functioning as a pestilence by spinning yarns of a glorified myth of a woman, cause the deepest traumatic wounds in the mind of a woman, who both biologically and emotionally are more sensitive when compared to the male. This often shatters her where she is forced to internalize and identify herself with the concept of the 'misfits' in the 'same world' and this becomes a spar to the tragedy which awaits her in the form of larger exploitations. This badly executed judgment, from the male world, lacking even a glimmer of perspicacity, forces a woman to return to a world of her own, where her emptiness and frustration merge and where they seek but fail to find a shoulder to shed their sorrow.

The male dominated society has drawn a line of prohibitions social, economic, cultural and even religious, for the female and if the female ever makes an attempt to get an access into the world of a 'male experience' it will be viewed as an outrageous act of transgression, as all the hurdles created by the society has been crumbling down before the fabricated myth of the male and he is petrified to the extend of dictating verdict for taboo transgression, thus making the life, for a woman, a really terrifying experience. The home spun life style of a woman, mainly centered round the concept of a family, often through the interferences of the male doctrines and dogmas come to have an experience of a labyrinth, where mostly she is destined to fumble and tremble to the point of being sneered at by enthusiastic spectator constituted mainly of the male folk. The psychological dilemmas that a woman confronts, in her day today life may lead her to a state of eccentricity where the burdens of loss haunts her even in her never- to be rosy life and here each episode of her life triggers off a tragic sequence for her. Woman often defends many of the psychological as well as cultural excavations into her life, intended to place woman at the receiving end through the smoldering of her historic position in the social strata, through the brand name engraved on her psyche i.e. 'defenseless'. Often patriarchy tend to perceive woman as socially hated, economically neglected and culturally barren and this identity, the first step in the process of enslavement denies her free access into the mainstream social life. This discrepancy between the male and female identity, according to Monalisa Changkija, requires a munificent validation, may be not to prove anything or to gain something, but only to concretize in a woman the worth and value of her identity.

The ripples of the self-assertion of Monalisa Changkija, as a woman, who is destined to receive the legacy of humiliation from the male folk, can be found moving through the surface of her poetry, hiding beneath it the larger currents of a revolt against the social situations responsible for it. Monalisa Changkija's poetry, being highly concerned of social situations and the role of one, especially that of a woman, in such a context, can never be fully digested by one, if he is unaware of the scurrilous attack on woman, as a scrumptious edible as there are some pricking thorns, not to pain but to partake in their pangs, hidden beneath the surface level charm. The very purpose of the composition of her poems is laid bare before the readers in the preface to the volume *Weapons of Words on Pages of Pain*, and here we experience the fragmentation process in the psychological life of a woman and the rive psyche of the female resulting from the crooked stratagem adopted by the patriarchy an oppressive measure. Monalisa Changkija says:

> The first part of this collection *Weapons of Words on Pages of Pain* and 'To Whom it may Concern' reflects some of my thoughts on battered and abused women, on domestic violence and on women's ability to rise above the 'second class citizenry'. Yes I am empathizing with and also crying out at the same time along with women who have suffered and continue to suffer in a discriminate society. I have however experienced domestic violence, memories of which are deeply etched in my mind and the pain still in my heart... no matter how hard we try to push them into the darkest corner of our minds and cupboards, the problem exists and one will have to open one's eyes from the core of the heart to see it.... (*Das. 2008:123-124)*

Here Monalisa Changkija expresses her deep concern, as a sharer of the psyche residue of the class of women, over the social tendency to place women on the 'back seat' through the series of shenanigans, and to applaud the oppressive mentality of the male who boast of a rich pedigree of mutual respect and recognition. In parts of *Weapons of Words on Pages of Pain*, the poet focuses on the plight of battered and abused women, who are gifted to rise but for a discriminating society. By way of physique, men are stronger, but intellectually women are superior:

> In a world where man is the boss his....
>
> Man's inadequacies
>
> And insecurities
>
> Speak in the
>
> Language of violence (*WoWoPoP:* 4)

The status of a woman is reduced to nothingness. The poet writes:

Children call them 'Mother'
Society defines them 'women' (*WoWoPoP:* 5)

There is irony questioning how much weight and respect a woman has been given. The inner turmoil of the gentlest species of mankind is surfaced, a universal question. Monalisa Changkija portrays the submission of a female, through her silence, of course not a choice from many, but one and the only one placed before her, by the male and the preference of him, to the unbridled and out pouring passions and opinions of the male in the poem "If Only":

If only I could tell you what I believe
But you want to hear only
What you want to hear
So I remain silent .....
And I really wouldn't ask you
To step out of your comfort zone
You'll not survive *(MM: 16)*

Here, a diagnosis has been attempted by the female obviously to the discomfiture of the male, regarding the male fraility, a term often and again placed, rather misplaced with the female. She trawls through the attributive values the male, mostly a donation from the part of the patriarchal society, in order to seek out a rendezvous, where ultimately the male and female identities conjoin on the common footing of their failings and comes out with the tragic conclusion, as far as a man is concerned, that once out of touch with the comfy existence, what awaits him, crouching on his way is nothing but devastations. Every woman's life portrays the effects of male chauvinism as her success and superiority stands somewhere beyond the digestion and tolerance of the male, since he views it from a male perspective, as a pasting. Mostly a woman's life, according to Monalisa Changkija, gets itself sandwiched between the inhuman cruelties of patriarchy and her social and household responsibilities though attempts have been made by her to answer certain questions of existence that were saying afore her. The profit that she often derives out of such a venture is more in the form of oppression, just meant to vanquish her to answer his power and superiority through which he will be able to soar high above others until the gratification of his 'vaulting ambition'. Monalisa Changkija shows how even love becomes an oppressive and exploitative means, (which actually should lead to the cementing of relationships and emotional bonds) where it largely becomes a bondage. This rusting emotional ties, where love and allied emotions and the proper expression of which in accordance with the demand of situations is portrayed by Monalisa Changkija in the following lines and frowns at the slipshod attitude of the society towards love:

> This cannot be an offering
> Of apologies
> Because I cannot forgive
> Anyone who has taken
> So much of me
> And contributed
> So generously
> To the erosion
> Of the earlier me
> All in the name of love
> And other such sentiments
> Culminating always
> In my imprisonment within
> Emotional relationships *(WoWoPoP: 23)*

The existential dilemmas of a woman, etched with submissiveness and sufferings, in a heightened, intolerable state, breaking all blockades, manifests itself as a volcanic eruption and at that moment all attempts of enticements, may fail. Monalisa Changkija advocates not a woman, who is a silent sufferer fulfilling all the requirements of a traditional woman in tune with the patriarchal notions and living at the depth of servility. The picture the poet draws of a woman, seems to be a contrary one to that portrayed by Arundhati Roy, through Mammachi, in *The God of Small Things (1997)*. There Arundhati Roy, attempts an immaculate portrayal of a typical Indian woman and her plight in the familial context, a microcosm of the larger society. Roy says:

> At pappachis' funeral Mammachi cried and her contact lenses slid around her eyes. Ammu told the twins that Mammachi was crying more because she was used to him than because she loved him. She was used to...being beaten...human beings were creatures of habit and it was amazing to find of things they could get used to.... Being beaten with brass vases were the least of them. *(1997: 50)*

Here, Mammachi is a picture of a silent sufferer having a stilting and suffocating story of losses to tell and only the realizations of the fallacy regarding her freedom around which a woman's life is being erected, cause open a safety outlet from the slumber in which women were immersed for ages and which of course made them being auctioned in accordance with the interests of patriarchy, has to be brought about through blasting the shell of passivity in which each woman finds a comfy zone. The necessity of such a counter-productive reaction to the selfish, uncouth behavior of the male becomes the thematic concern of Monalisa Changkija in the following lines, which becomes an artistic celebration of Feminism:

> Immersed as I am
> In situations overwhelming
> I refuse to acknowledge
> The barred doors around me

Some where there is a window
With hinges not too taut
For my feminine strength and will
To open and escape *(WoWoPoP: 25)*

Pain, and suffering, to a woman, arrive not in singles, but in battalions, throttling her, mostly assuming the form of frustrations experienced due to simple dreams that are shattered and unfulfilled aspirations of simple joys en masse constituting a 'home' for her. This mélange of diverse pangs, experienced by a woman, in her personal as well as social life, scribble the history of a woman, which often will be a sad tale of defeat and desperation. The unfathomable depth between the expectations of a woman, not far off reality and the actual attainment possibility of it seems to be the thematic concern of Monalisa Changkija in the poem "Field of Babys' Breaths":

Alas, this is not to be
I was cut and created
From a different type of stone
To meet the needs of
A different type of times
Times that denied me
The chance to sing and sew
Cook and indulge in floral delights
As women are expected to *(MM: 14)*

3. Conclusion

Monalisa Changkija, with a scholastic vibrancy, undertakes the exhibition of the sorry spectacle of a woman and in this attempt her attention does not merely filter through the 'female' and the 'feminine' rather her all encompassing vision as that of a maverick artist sumptuously roams through different dimensions of human, animal and even natural life to find materials to supplement it, where she, frequently, pays witness to the scuffle between natural forces and human beings but above all between human beings, both man and woman.

A reader, once enraptured by the poetry of Monalisa Changkija who, having the power to decode unlike a valerine street in a greater sound may be that of a stifled whimper, even from silence, can find a world of eco-Feminism opening before him. In the poem "Mist over Brahmaputra", Monalisa Changkija fashions a farrago of resemblances between the female and the river, Brahmaputra, the sun of Brahma, the sustainer and it becomes an epitome of the eco-feminist sensibility of Monalisa Changkija. Here the poet, depicting the female and the river streaming through similar experiences, speaks of the unquenchable thirst of Brahmaputra for sun and the unending waiting for him, through which, of course the needs and requirements of a woman:

> To celebrate the sights, scents and sounds
> And the strength in my solitary self
> And allow time to heal
> These self destructive tendencies
> That sometimes buzz around my head
> As they do over Brahma's son.
> And like Brahma's son I wait
> For the serenades of the sun
> To soak up the mist over Brahmaputra *(MM: 4)*

The dream and desire of a woman to ramble through the little path ways of nature, which according to her expectations, would make possible the advent of greater ramifications, which in turn will be a blessing in disguise to her anguished heart. Here also the identification sought by a woman's heart, with that of the elements of the nature proclaims the eco-feminist temperament of Monalisa

Changkija. When a woman is hoodwinked to dance in tune, with the patriarchy, playing the role of a piper, where the individuality of a woman gets razzed, she dreams of heights, where little birds robustly engage themselves in all sorts of rollicking endeavors. This eco-feminist element finds expression in the following lines:

> No I do not feel privileged
> With perfumes and paints
> And find warmth in
> Silk, satin and laces
> No I will not be blinded
> And cannot be bought
> By black sequined dresses
> I have set my sights
> Towards the skies
> To swirt with swallows
> And chip with sparrows. *(WoWoPoP: 26)*

A woman caught up in an intricate nexus of psychological imbroglio, which places her in a border line situation, where larger questions on the forward functioning of life, which in the case of a woman, due to pressurizations from the nook and corners of daily life, mostly experiences a backward pull, arise to dismantle her tranquil and serene life. Here Monalisa Changkija provides an option to the modern world having a meretricious Socialism in all spheres of life, even in the treatment of the female, and thus a unified synergy of the male and female in each step of life, according to her, would, mitigate the pangs of the female. This ardent belief of Changkija invades into the heart of the generation through the following lines:

> And I wowed rather
> We soar and sing together

But if you don't reach out
To hold my hand
I'd still break the bars and fly
Though in my heart I may cry *(WoWoPoP: 29)*

Thus Monalisa Changkija as a poet of feminist fervor, looks at the plight of modern woman, sometimes through nature, and sighs at the maelstrom of diverse pricking thorns in her life and propagates a 'Socialism in Feminism' which to the male and the female would provide a common ground to advance hand in hand, just as Amelia Earhart stated,

> Women must try to do things as men have tried. When they fail, their failure must be but a challenge to others. *(Davies. 2006: 110)*

We may say, that Monalisa's poetry has a universal appeal. She does not give up all her hope, she is optimistic that one day gender stratification would come to an end, for she believes in the power of the weapon she utilizes:

Ah, but you forget
My weapons of words
I leave behind
On these pages of pain. (*WoWoPoP:* 12)

Monalisa has selected the best of words in their best of forms in the poem "Walking Alone". Most of the verses in this poem have just two words each. The poem is very carefully written in such a way that even the most careless reader would be provoked to react to gender discrimination. Her verses have the power to reach untouched corners of the heart in an inexplicable way. Though this poem has eleven verses, it has just one single meaning. It is better to live alone than with a man who sees no difference between animals and wives. Living in a society that constantly spread rumors, about single woman living alone is a hard task. It requires a lot of will power and courage. And yet she says it would be like life in the paradise for those women who are battered:

Walking alone
Through the
Passage of time
And falling into
The abyss of
The irredeemable
Would be paradise,
Than living in
"Sacred matrimony"
With anyone
Who sees no
Difference between
Animals, servants
And wives. (*WoWoPoP:* 9)

Monalisa's poetry reveals the history of not only the Naga society but the entire North-East India. If Socialism is her password, Monalisa Changkija has excelled in placing before every reader, social grief that need to be borne together by every individual, so that for a reformation, and the need for lending a ear to the female species of mankind, which craves to heard and loved. Monalisa makes readers believe that Feminism stands for gender equality, independence and empowerment of women. Women tend to write about women, so that their works are a reasonable place to look, for the depictions of female life. Boldly, the poet as a liberal feminist, through her poems has offered accessibility to women, to the public realm. She celebrates the feminist aspects of the human being which has been depreciated and ascribed to women. Her poems, brave that women are no longer 'Women of a thousand tears.' Monalisa's poetry is woman's transition from total silence to articulation in a revolutionary revision. As Robert Greene declared,

> Do not accept the rules that society foists on you. Recreate yourself by forging a new identity òne that commands attention.....mastering, your own image rather than letting others define it for you. Incorporate dramatic devised into your public gestures and actions – your power will be enhanced and your character will seem larger than life. *(Greene.1999: p.191).*

Monalisa Changkija's poems have power and character, looming affront each individual, to reflect, articulate and promote specific beliefs and values.

5

Romance of Socialism and Feminism in the Poetic Works of Robin S. Ngangom

Robin S. Ngangom is a bilingual poet, who writes in English and Manipuri. He is a significant writer in the literature of North-East India, and has to his credit three volumes of poetry:

1. *Time's Crossroads (1994)*
2. *Words and the Silence (1998)*
3. *The Desire of Roots (2006).*

1. Socialism in Robin S. Ngangom's Poetry

Robin S. Ngangom describes his poetry as "mostly autobiographical, written with the hope of enthusing readers with my communal or carnal life", the life of a politically discriminated - against, historically – overlooked individual from the nook of a third world country." He adopts a simple, but elegant style which is scarcely found in the literature of the North-East India. He is compelled to respond to different socio-economic factors that threaten the normal life of the common people of the region. The role of the poet is clear to him, in this ongoing "reign of terror" as that of a witness and chronicler.

There are not many poets in India, who write with

more passion than Robin S. Ngangom. He is very much aware of the state of anarchy and horror that has distorted the lives of his people. Robin S. Ngangom after having recognized the somnambulist mental state of the people in the 21st century tries to communicate the incommunicable, meant to wake them up from the stupor of a comfy island like existence, and to provide them with the first lessons of Socialism so that he could, though a strenuous task, channelize the lives of the people, at least a little bit towards a progressive social existence. He realized the resilience of the people, but was never unaware of the traumatic effects generated by the guns. In his viewpoint the wailing social situation, fails to witness the advent of the socialist order of the society and for its establishment the culture of the gun and ammunitions has to be relegated to that of the culture of a white flag, i.e. of peace. The dream of a nation, which in actuality, for them, is far removed from reality but not unattainable if attempted to grab, unveils itself through the words of Robin S. Ngangom in the poem "We are not ready for the hand of peace." Here the antithetical and ambivalent attitude of the people, that expresses itself in the form of socio-cultural conflicts and where the uproar of the guns become the alphabet of the people, Robin S. Ngangom takes a participant's role, sharing and at the same time caring for them in this particular poem. Their expectation never borders on an unassailable material or monetary progress, rather their simple dreams, often seen as silly ones by those who never need to have such dreams, are centered on 'carte blanche' where individuality gets itself asserted:

> peace without fear of another vicious tomorrow
> is what we search, and not the false dust of
> the seven brandished swords who guard our backs.
> We have exhausted springtide flowers to plant
> in the muzzle of guns and
> What we desire is the witness of still winds

We wish to hear the melodious laugh
Of the cheeks of children, the eyes of beloved
It is not the vile mockery of devils we hope to hear again. *(TDOR: 89)*

In "Poetry in the time of terror" he says, that his poetry springs from the cruel contradictions of his native-land. Manipur boasts of its talents in theater, cinema, dances and sports. But how could one trust his own people who would entrust corruption, aid terrorism and distribute drugs to their children? "The lost generation of Manipur" is a vindication of the social degradation that is creeping into the society he loves so much. His people cannot be happy because they have abandoned their roots:

How can they if they cannot
Fornicate, nor dance,
Nor sing with the innocence
Of their abandoned roots? *(WATS: 26)*

The social consciousness of the poet does not allow him to keep silent, at the terrible things happening in Manipur, his homeland. The poem "Nativeland" speaks of his people in simple but powerful words:

First came the scream of the dying
In a bad dream, then the radio report
And a newspaper six shot dead, twenty five
Houses razed, sixteen beheaded with hands tied
Behind their backs inside a church
As the days crumbled, and the victors
And their victims grew in number,
I hardened inside my thickening hide,
Until I lost my tenuous humanity. (*TDOR:* 81)

Robin S. Ngangom exhibits a fine balance between

realism and reflection. He is a poet of the here and the now. The modern society admires the rich, even an upstart is admired by the people no matter how they make money. The poet is worried about the loss of values in the society. In "Values" he realizes:

You say with all my acquired learning
A mechanic, a clerk, class three officers
Earn much more than me. Perhaps
It is no use. It is futile (*WATS: 64)*

The poet means to say that it is futile to run after money, riches and the worldly possessions. He sympathizes in the same poem with those who:

earn like a dog
and eat like a horse! (*WATS: 64)*

The duress under which, individuals act and where life transforms itself into a picture of mere duplicity due to the cultural degradation occurring as a result of the social degeneration, excreted by a social class who consider themselves to be of paramount importance, makes the society which is a unified and unifying force as the term indicates, divisible, culminating in the birth of a social group called the 'pareabs' or the outcasts. Robin S. Ngangom, through his poetry, attempts a riposte to those who vouch for the supremacy of an autocratic system, which according to him, would wipe away vestiges, of the socialist order that waged war against one's own fellow being to concretize supremacy over the other. The bareness of the present when placed against the fertility of the past intensifies the deluge of sorrows, as it airs a number of losses and absences, especially, the absence of Socialism. The word 'tomorrow' speaks of a great deliverance from the shackles of the past and a wiping off especially that of memory, which is a gratuitous source of pain. Even while unsure of the future awaiting them with its fund of mysteries, they invariably keep their head erect looking straight into the future with mutilated dreams.

In "From the Book of Grievance's" Robin S. Ngangom places before the reader such a social situation of exasperation and expectation, and in turn it becomes a contrast between the socialist past and the present devoid of any traces of Socialism:

> Today with grief sitting on our hearts
> we will sing of clouds that do not come home
> we will sing the songs of those
> banished in the mountains
> we will drink deep from bamboo mugs
> and wipe memory from our lips
> from the trajectory of our dark deeds
> our days are bound for destinations
> in unknown galaxies of time *(TC: 45)*

Robin S. Ngangom is highly concerned of such a social phenomenon and through his poetry, he lays bare before the readers, the exploitative tendencies of the society which creates a gulf between the rich and the poor and which exists forever as a never to be neglected fact of the day. In the poem "I am sorry to see Poetry in Chains" Robin S. Ngangom speaks of the plight of the present day Socialism and this portrayal depicts the imponderable repercussions it can have in the society in the future, failing to extricate the poor from the web in which they are caught and from which they aspire for a redemption the poet says:

> Follow and strep that ragged girl
> who brings milk barefoot in the morning
> in the pounding rain
> with an umbrella full of holes.
> Way lay the grass cutter and flog him

Just to see if he bleeds like the others

Let us wage war on innocent things

On nature's children, on sons of the soil

With knives, sticks and stones

My love, do not let me hurt you

These words, these hands

Are drunk with fear and anger (*WATS: 69)*

The fear and the anger, about which the poet speaks in a melancholic fervor is something which is borne out of the failure to install Socialism, the presence of which, would have brought about an oomph in the social life and would not have left the marginalized in a quandary. The figment regarding Socialism, purposefully generated with the assistance of all the paraphernalia of the society, completely entices the downtrodden to be participants in social life, even amidst the temperamental treatment meted out to them by the racing predominant culture. Robin S. Ngangom dresses up his attitudes regarding the collapsing social stability in poetic diction, to give it as much protection as possible from the state of a mere 'sedimentation', which would be seen with, a greater suspicious as socio-cultural or religio-political doctrines and dogmas fails in the appreciation of the corrections, rather they attempt a downright negation of what is spoken of against their attitudinal exercises. He realizes that in the present day, life in order to lead it forward in a peaceful manner, requires not only ones own effort rather it demands attention and attempt from many who directly or indirectly encircle one in the social context. Socialism, having the purpose to provide one with optimum happiness, gets itself polluted and Robin S. Ngangom along with Nora Ephron, the famous essayist holds the view, while nostalgically summating over the past that,

> We have lived through the era when happiness
> was a warm puppy, and the era when happiness

> was a dry martini and now we have come to the era when happiness is 'knowing what your uterus looks like.' *(Scholes, Robert et al. 2004: 7).*

He realizes the sacrificial circumstances, in which many paid homage to freedom and peace and especially for a socialist cause, through there lives and with which they expected to attain the highest, realm of Socialism not for themselves, but for those who commemorate them, even in bereavement. This paradoxical situation of an outrageous act is well exemplified in the poem "Two":

> while you fight for a selfless cause
> and make a fugitive of your life
> you also burn the flower of youth
> with the pious fire in your veins
> but our families have been herded
> and from loved ones severed *(TC : 50)*

At the heart of all, poetry is the idea of persuasion and aesthetic appreciation and many a poetry wears its heart on its sleeve and with much boldness declares its purpose but a few poets, often constituted of the best of the group, hide such a purpose beneath the veneer of the stylistic and linguistic aspects of poetry. Robin S. Ngangom is a writer having affinities and correspondences, with other forms of literature and largely shares an impulse toward a metaphoric depiction, but not in complex terms. The power to record faithfully is almost an automatic legacy of this particular writer and what he tries to represent is the unfulfilled yearnings in the human heart. By constructing a rhythmic resonance through the meditation selection of the images and diction, Robin S. Ngangom robs the heart of the readers, by exhibiting a flavor for the socialist order, which in a way adorns his poetry. In his fascination for a socialist society, where all the demarcations disappear, Robin S. Ngangom speaks of a very transparent Socialism, that break all the boundaries even that of racial segregation.

He finds a rare Socialism there. In "Poetry" he in an orotund tone endorses such an aspiration and finds poetry a means to such an end:

All I wanted was to sing
with the mystical sparrows
but only a murder of crows
nest in my throat at drawn.
I wanted to harvest words
Which grow on their own, words
Which die without tawdry funerals
Of creepers and vines, stars and stones,
Wisdom and folly, flowers and moss (*TDOR: 17)*

The suffocation, a contemporaneous phenomenon in the 'fret and fever' of the modern living, and which provides life a slovenly appearance, sends its roots deep down into the core of the poet's heart. Even then, Ngangom attempts a kind of topiary through poetry, while he sings of a future, which is going to be a contrast to the present day war-weary situation, and which will be one of a scintillating era of Socialism where:

everyone, with the poet may sing
Let our travel-weary eyes
drink once more from our sweet springs (*WATS : 19)*

Ngangom is a candid and brave writer, who has the caliber to use his weapon effectively. He is daringly frank and brave in his poetical works. He does not mind whom he hurts by speaking out the truth. He points his pen to the individuals and his words are directed to the deepest nook of the reader's heart. The nostalgic element in many of his poems is not just like the mere homesickness of an adolescent, but the pouring out of a non-belligerent individual for the peaceful years that were, and probably will return some time or other in the future. Every verse of his poetry reveals his magnanimity in one way or other. He creates a world of his own and invites the readers to that world, which is half-real and half-mysterious. Connotations are as frequent as and even more meaningful than denotations in some of the works of Ngangom. One of the chief characteristics of Robin S. Ngangom's manner of writing poetry is his economy of words. Choosing a minimum number of words he skillfully conveys a variety of thoughts. "It Has Become Dangerous to Love You" is one of the poems included in *The Desire of Roots.* In the second stanza of this poem he states trenchantly:

> Everywhere poets only want to live make love and sing (*TDOR* : 39)

Here the sole purpose of a poet's life in his view is explained. To live here does not mean simply to exist. The perspicuous meaning is to be active, in other words to take active part in the different social issues, to intensify the knowledge revolution to watch and to listen, to extend a soothing touch to the petrified, to understand and to be a harbinger of change, for in the poem "The Dead" he writes:

> Wolfing and breathing is not life (*TDOR:* 82)

Robin S. Ngangom is a lyric poet. Variety, simplicity, charm and beauty that cluster around in his poetry are the most prominent characteristic of his diction. Many a time, his diction does not lead the reader of his poetry to any definite conclusions but distracts them. At times his ideas converge and other times diverge. It is a difficult task to predetermine where he intends to arrive at; it is all of a sudden that the writer reveals his direction. At times he affects metaphysics too. In poems such as "I am Unable to Explain", Ngangom deals with some of the most pertinent questions in the life of those living in the Northeastern parts of India:

I am unable to explain to my daughter
What this war of freedom is
Or the meaning of liberation
That most hopeful of words. (*TDOR:* 91)

Ngangom gives the reader sufficient reasons as to why he is a poet. In the poem entitled "Poetry" he gives the reasons for being a poet:

Like the great poets
Pardoned by time
I wanted to gather words
From arrows necked in a turquoise sky. (*TDOR:* 34)

He wants 'rainy words' and 'pebbly words' to fashion his thoughts and to give life to his imaginations. There is a desperate need to be understood and to be accepted in his verse. The poet's desire is to be in constant conversation with his readers' even years after he has left the stage. Death should not be a barrier for him in communicating with the readers. The fears of being misunderstood and forgotten are evident in the following verses:

I want to describe myself again and again
To people who do not know me.
That is why I always look for paper and ink
Even in the midst of terrible loss,
Or, a dangerous illness.
Because someone said
The spoken word flies But the written word stays
(*Unpublished*)

The poet does not require a word of appreciation from the reader; simply being read is being appreciated and understood for him. The reader cannot fail to understand the poet, not merely because of the diction and the style but because of a strong rapport which the writer makes with his readers.

Some of the poems in the collection *The Desire of Roots* are concerned with pertinent social issues like: Why peace, elude us? Why do people behave in the way they do? Should people weep for others? Who has prestige? Who lacks it? Who holds power? Who does not? Perhaps the most touching elegy ever written in the history of the North-East poetry is "To Pacha" by Robin S. Ngangom. Pacha Meitei was one of the finest Manipuri writers, who passed away at the age of forty-six. He was hounded as a drunkard and a madman, during his final years, and he died in extreme poverty in the year 1990. The poet was deeply pained not only because of his sad demise, but also because of the ingratitude that the people of Manipur showed, to this great writer after his death. The irresponsibility of the society which was dearly loved by Pacha, is criticized by the poet irrefutably in the poem. The poet laments the truculent young generation of his homeland, who are pre-occupied with persecuting the pregnant women and children, have no tears to shed for innocent Pacha's lonely alcoholic-end. Nihilism has been adopted by the young boys as their modern philosophy. The parents have failed to impart values to their children, and they have turned amoral. The poet weeps at the plight of his homeland. His love for Pacha is deeply felt all through the poem, though he addresses Pacha as consummate madman. The poet's desire to open the hearts of his people is felt in the second stanza of the poem in a significant way:

> There are no more tears to shed
> In this withered country where they
> Kill pregnant women and children; its
> Nipples have long gone dry, and leering
> Death walks your home land. And why should
> Anyone weep for your lonely alcoholic end?

Young boys and soldiers are butchering each
Other by the dozen, in the hills, the angry
Streets, day after day, and too many heroes
And villains are not worth remembering at all.
is callous, Pacha, in the land of your
innocent birth. (*TDOR:* 34)

The religious outlook of the poet unveils itself in the poem "Prayer to the one who Sleeps above." The poet praises God for a number of reasons. The elements of liberation theology are found in the poem. The poet's expression of gratitude to the Almighty differs from that of others, because of the fact that he is grateful to God for what a normal believer thinks, is a sin. Sex is considered a sin by many Indians, and wine is regarded as the source of all evils. Nobody would like to speak in-favor of these two things. The poet has courageously expressed his gratitude to God for them. Here the poet's goal must be to mock the hypocrisy of the people who secretly enjoy sex and wine and at the same time deny them in public:

You have my thanks for
The sinless pleasure of my flesh,
The mystical formula of wine,
The feasts of the earth. (*TC:* 44)

The poet seeks answer to the question why peace eludes us? People are at war with shadow warriors. Fraternity has given way to frenzy. The people offended the old gods they were worshiping and began worshiping new gods of greed and narcotic death. The poem "To the blind the deaf" deals with this issue. The focal point of this poem is the issue of peace which is a distant dream, taking into account the cruel contradictions of the land. The poem analyses tradition, culture, philosophy and perhaps a little of wickedness around:

Their descendants still fight today-
With shadow warriors.
For offending the old gods
They were cursed, to be turned
Into a blind and deaf people
Worshiping new gods of greed
And narcotic death. (*TC:* 58)

The poet states the reason for today's sufferings and then concludes the poem with a prophecy that is true with the present generation:

Surely peace will elude us. (*TC:* 59)

Modernism in the poetry of Robin S. Ngangom is not a complete break with the past. The past events, experiences and occurrences are seen in a new light i.e. the light of modernism. The poet draws his ideas, characters and symbols from the well of indigenous traditions, which are seldom incomprehensible to the readers. The poet fully exploits the folk traditions he grew up with. The rich oral literature of the Khasis, casts its impact on the poet. This is evident when he sings:

I told you the stories of old
On soft Sundays, of manic Raitong
And Ka Likai. Only the stones of unknown gorges
Weep for them, I said. (*Unpublished*)

The above quoted lines project, Ngangom not only as a modernist with a deeply felt love for the past, but socialist who stands against social and gender stratification. The poet conceives the folklore stories and broods over them, before he converts them into verses that have the power to awaken the collective unconscious of a race.... a race that constantly wreak havoc upon itself. The simple but forceful diction adopted by the poet, in versifying the folk stories cannot fail in contributing, to the unification of souls and bringing about harmony. The social commitment of Ngangom reflects itself in the manner in which he treats his subjects. One of the most praise-worthy poems from the collection *Time's Crossroads* is "At Noh Ka Likai's" (The Leap Of Ka Likai). This poem is a lyric with elegiac qualities. The gruesome murder of the child and the eating of its flesh by the women, do not find a place in the poem. Yet the poem opens in such a way that even the most heartless reader would be startled at once, for the words pierce through a corner of the readers' heart:

> We passed weeping stones
> Silent faces of stone wrinkled with pain
> And a young wind scouring the gorge
> I descend the broken course
> Of a shriveled stream to the green pool
> Sunk by the waterfall. (*TC:* 60)

The poem is written in free verse, abandoning all the conventional rules of poetry writing. Reading the poem brings to mind the Marxian philosophy that the goal is more important than the way:

> To day's fall Khasi beloved come with me.
> Among the hushed pines tell us again
> Who have forgotten
> Of evil buried in the sun of man.
> Speak with your silver hair
> Above dark green waters, your
> Shimmering feet among pebbles. (*TC:* 60)

It is better to consider most of the poems contained in the collection *Time's Crossroads*, as the poet's attempt to be a part of the fight against anti–Socialism, women stratification, mechanization and commoditization of human activities. War and terror have left a lasting mark on the poet's mind that he introspects and realizes that the natives of this land are as responsible for the present situation of the land as other people. The poet does not care about the acceptability of his thoughts but only about its relevance. The harsh reality of life that is witnessed by the people living in the North-East takes predominance in the poem "Arms will flower here too." The social concern of the poet is reflected in this lyric too. The poet's love for nature is also refracted in the poem. The poet probes the cause, for the prevailing unhappy life in the hills and on getting the answer he points his finger at the readers saying - you too are one of the conspirators. Being inactive is a crime, for that leads to the 'stealing of peace from these gentle hills':

We are all guilty
Like men all over the earth,
We know why poverty
Had walked the countryside naked,
We have seen hunger flowering
From bamboos in the villages.
We wanted peace for ourselves
By stealing the peace
Of these gentle hills. (*TC:* 52)

Ngangom is an audacious and venturesome poet. He experiments with a variety of themes and triumphs over them. He daringly romances with intricate issues such as Socialism and Feminism. Socialism as mirrored in the poetry of Robin S Ngangom is not a mere political and economic theory, advocating state ownership and control of means of production distribution and exchange. It is not even a social system based on any of the above mentioned factors rather it is a way of living. Whether a person lives not only as he wishes, but also let others live as they wish. For Ngangom, Socialism is the flow of human goodwill, a spirit that has to be experienced. His poetry exposes a society that is under moral and social threat. The fast vanishing long held values disappoint him not because he is a traditionalist without individual talent, but because of the rapture he has for the society. "Native land" is a poem included in the collection *The Desire of Roots*. While reading it, even without any predetermined intention, distinct images begin to flow into the mind of the reader. The horrible acts of violence are portrayed in such a way, that the reader is left with no option but to empathize, with those at the receiving end:

First came the scream of the dying
In a bad dream, then the radio report,
And a newspaper: six shot dead, twenty five
Houses razed, sixteen beheaded with hands tied
Behind their backs inside a church..... (*TDOR:* 81)

The simplicity of these lines is sufficient to prove the potential of the poet. The poet has not adhered to the use of any figures of speech, yet the style is elegant, the words are pregnant with meaning. Real life is portrayed just as it is seen in the North-Eastern part of India, without any exaggeration. The underlying spirit of this poem and many other poems of Robin S. Ngangom is full of feminist ideas. A deeply felt love is reflected in almost all his poems especially for human beings- the crown of creations. His poetry aims at a bloodless revolution. The verses infuse a kind of love, into the hearts of the readers, a kind, because it is not aimed at attaining anything except peace with the help of the verses that are arranged like the phyllotaxy on a stem. As the reader shifts from page to page, this love for the humanity flows into the reader. In the poem "Body" he says, it is not time that is the enemy of the body, but 'the mind with its dark pledges'. Yet the body resists and is essentially capable of finding solutions to any number of problems:

Remove a hand and the foot starts painting
Deny eyes and figures are already on the keys.

These lines are sufficient proof to reveal clearly, Ngangom's deeply internalized politics. He has imbibed all the better parts of a lyric poet, though he is an extremely self conscious writer.

Human beings are born with latent urges, abilities, capacities, interests, aptitudes and other personality traits. The prime concern of the poet seems to be to penetrate into the human heart. In-depth knowledge about diverse psychological and sociological characteristics of human nature is exhibited in the poetry of Ngangom. He adopts an all absorbing approach and treats his thoughts as his subjects. That is why Socialism and Feminism have gained predominance in the poetical works of Ngangom. The poet is a social being and so the wounds that hurt the society hurts the poets too. "Revolutionaries":

Before they used terror when things were beginning to go out
Of control and people showed aberrant behaviour.
Revolutionaries had asked poets in their lower ranks to compose
Patriotic songs for a country which cannot be found on any map.(*TDOR:* 54)

"Revolutionaries" is a lyric poem written in blank verse. The tremendous impact of the underground factions on the normal life of the common people in the North-East region of India is mirrored in this poem. The poem has two parts. The first part is written entirely in past tense. Every stanza of the first part of this poem begins with the word 'Before'. The poet gives a vivid description of the social set up that existed 'before' in his region. People fighting tooth and nail 'for a country which cannot be found on any map, has made life a worthless thing in the region. The social consciousness of the poet enables him to relate his past experiences amicably. He tells the reader the fact that, many of the so-called revolutionaries go under the ground for selfish reasons. Even innocent young people are attracted to the anti-social groups and ruthlessly do any heinous activity:

> Before he became the sharpshooter of a revolutionary band my
> Childhood friend smelled of straw and cattle, and then one day
> He bridled a horse and rode it hard through a busy marketplace
> Scattering customers and traders alike like straw in a gale (*TDOR* : 54)

The second part ,of "Revolutionaries" which in the present tense gives a clear picture of the present day North-East. When the 'revolutionaries are not around they become butts of fun'. People begin to discuss about unimportant things as usual. This ability of human beings to forget is stressed by Ngangom. Horror and hope occur simultaneously in the "Revolutionaries" horror while narrating the horrible past events and hope for a peaceful secured society amid the contemporary happenings. Social change occurs only through public awareness. Thus the poet strives to create a socially consciousness society. He often adopts humor as a weapon for spreading public awareness. In the "Revolutionaries" too the reader comes across an element of humor:

> The roving story then was of a wastrel who went home after midnight
> Because he had wasted all his time with his lay about friends
> Around a fire one later night. He had to cross a walled house

Guarded by furious dogs to reach his home when the owner of
The house who was woken up by the dogs asked who goes
There? The wastrel found his wits and replied, 'In the service
Of the motherland' in a solemn voice as one would expect a Revolutionary to reply. (*TDOR:* 55)

Humour is not employed by Ngangom for its own sake, but to direct a thought into the reader's intellectual self. Does it mean that Ngangom is a didactic writer? Not really, he does not intend to teach the readers but wishes that the readers are taught. He doesn't give the message but wants the message to be understood. Keeping social welfare as the chief aim, the poet uses humor as a tool to attain this goal.

All major social issues have been featured in the poems of Ngangom. Social stratification has injured the poet to compose one of the most beautiful poems, titled "Middle Class Blues." The middle class people have to struggle for a dual purpose. Their chief intention is not to fall back into the lower class, at the same time they struggle to reach the aristocratic ways of life. Money is the determining factor, so the middle class man cannot afford to be too luxurious. The poet rightly points out:

A middle class man
Wakes up on a middle class morning
And has his middle class tea and biscuits (*TDOR:* 84)

The middle class men are afraid of falling below the poverty line. This troubles his mind though 'on occasion' he may wear his single suit. Ngangom airs his views on issues relating to the marriage and love affairs of middle class people. The middle class people know quite well what they are expected to do. The poet has travelled through the middle class life absorbing the different aspects:

A middle class man merely wants to save his money
Troubling no one and expecting no trouble in return.
Though he fell in love during his pre-industrial youth
He eventually married a middle class bride
And dutifully buys his middle class fish
Constantly checking his middle class watch. (*TDOR:* 84)

The reader is lead not by an elegant rhyme scheme but, by carefully chosen and well organized diction into the midst of the middle class society. The social behaviour of a middle class man is predetermined. The poet condemns the majority of the middle class people, who are pre-occupied with saving money and so live a miserly life in spite of having sufficient money to live a comfortable life. Yet, it is his money that keeps a democracy well oiled, because he pays his war taxes and earthquake dues, without a murmur of dissent. Ngangom's direct experience with middle class people has paved the way for writing such a socially relevant poem as the 'middle class blues.' There may hardly be anyone who does not love his native land. The poet too loves his native land and is worried about the heinous acts, of the so called revolutionaries whom the government calls as terrorists. He weeps the loss of his tenuous humanity in the poem "Native land":

As the days crumbled and the victors
And their victims grew number,
I hardened inside my thickening hide
Until, lost my tenuous humanity. (*TDOR:* 81)

The element of realism in "Native Land" cannot be neglected. The poet has just mirrored what actually happens in the society. The North-Eastern part of India witnesses corruption, cold blood murder, theft and the like, almost everyday. The poet reveals the fact that common people have developed a dangerous attitude of ' I don't care any more.' This attitude is dangerous says the poet, because it leads to the loss of 'humanity.' Human beings have a better capacity to adapt themselves, to the changing environments than any other living being. The poet appeals not to the intellect of the readers, but to their emotions, for he knows that man is an emotional being and that only by appealing to the emotions of the people he can accelerate this silent, bloodless revolution of spreading peace into the human hearts. The poet is engaged in this social revolution, not with guns and other weapons, but with a deeply felt love for humanity. Years of waiting for a peaceful North-East tires him and he thinks loudly:

> I ceased thinking
> Of abandoned children inside blazing huts
> Still waiting for their parents. (*TDOR:* 81)

The horrible acts of violence, in the North-East India get global exposure through the poetry of eminent poets like Robin S. Ngangom. The revolutionaries set fire to the huts of the innocent villagers, maybe to get noticed, maybe to release their pent-up feelings. The poet is of the opinion that it is population at a loss, with what to do with itself that overruns the public places. He addresses a generation that has lost the aim of life in the poem "From the Book of Grievances."

2. Feminism in the Poetry of Robin S. Ngangom

Ngangom is not a feminist of the usual type with 'much ado about nothing.' He is a writer with a purpose. His love and concern for the stratified gender is reflected in 'At Noh Ka Likai's' in a much different way than in other works. The poet eternalizes Ka Likai in this poem with an amusingly fewer number of words. His concise diction speaks more than elegant speeches, from the pulpits for the liberation of women. The incident of Ka Likai's suicide is made the theme of this poem with an intention to open the mind of the society, towards the intolerable life that most women are living in our society.

In the modern world, a concept that evolved out as a result of a counter-movement and ever since its inception , till the present day, which has never assumed the status of a shibboleth , is of course Feminism, a shower to the parched feminine spirit. The megalomaniac tendencies of the patriarchy suppressing the female through physical, psychological, theoretical and even moral means, ensured the plight of the woman, who is cast into the ditches of sexism from where a revival and rejuvenation appear not an easy task. One of the significant key terms, that gained currency in the modern feminist discourse is of course the term "miserable miscalculations" and this terminology, when adequately examined, provide the sum total of a woman in the modern social background. But the irrepressible feminine spirit, through exhibiting the greatest signs of survival through a great endurance, demands kudos even from the foe, i.e. the 'male', patriarchy, while implanting a yoke, both physically and psychologically, on a woman, through a series of manipulative tactics , of which the woman may be unaware, exhibits his mastery over her even in brutal inhuman ways, where he actually degenerates into the state of a "nouveau riche", who is but an upstart and a fruition of snobbery having little sense or essence of his own. As a result of the stereotyping- as the fragile and the secondary- a woman experiences a process of "sedimentation" occurring there in her psyche, which would ultimately transform her to get identified with the role in which the patriarchy places her and often she finds the newly woven robe – of the "other" - a really comfy one from where she dislikes to be unwrapped.

Robin. S. Ngangom, in his poetry, subtly creates an unvarnished history of the suppression experienced by the female. The heartstrings of the poet, as he hearkens to the yells of the female and pays witness to the slew of struggles with which she is engaged in a perpetual conflict get opened up in the medium of poetry. The trepidation, surging through the mind of the female, resulting from the unmanly attitude of the patriarchal social codes towards the female, who is seen and branded as a wonky creature, has been shared by the poet. Patriarchy demands obeisance from the part of the female but at the same time the female is viewed by the male, ripping her off an identity and individuality, as a mere lascivious object, specially framed for his biological satisfaction. This obdurate attitude of the patriarchy as well as the sensitive simplicity of the female finds adequate representation in the poetry of Robin S. Ngangom. The concept of womanhood and the closely allied concept virginity, valued supreme but paid scarce respect and reverence in the lusty expectations, mostly occurring as futile, unreal dreams, find portrayal in the poem "Lessons". Here the poet unmasks the sensations and sensibilities of the female as she passes through the diverse stormy experiences in the course of her historic growth which in the eyes of the patriarchy is nothing but a biological growth naturally occurring. But Robin S. Ngangom like a mutinous writer, never circumscribed by the patriarchal notions, though biologically a part of that specific culture and tradition, discloses the pent-up emotions of the female, which find no outlet to extricate itself freely. He says:

> There was hard maidenhood
> Preserved with cold kisses
> and easy girls
> trying to borrow virginity
> for one solitary night.
> There were widows concealing
> quiet fears in urns
> and rich women comforted
> for the smallest pain

There were variations
of the same day
the same silent rain
and repetitive winters (*TC: 38)*

Robin S. Ngangom, while speaking in favor of the feminine cause, often brings in the imagery of the winter, which, according to him, may appear to be an eyesore and similar is the situation with the life of each woman whose existence, to the patriarchal norms, may be having the effect of a similar atmosphere and along with it the frigid, isolated existence of the woman too, find representation here. The paroxysm of ire, cast at the female, demolishes her to the core and even the riotous protests, may be from very few corners, consequently get subsided through the provocative proclamations of the male. "Cultural cannibalism" reigns in the contemporary society, making clamor of exploitation and amidst this the life of a woman gets sidelined and even her words are given only the status of 'fuddy-duddy' ideas. The psychological state of a woman- on the basis of which two divisions are possible – in the patriarchal society where she, sometimes stagger to the level of a collapse, is adequately interrelates in an essay title *Cocksure women and Hensure men* by D.H. Lawrence. Here the plight of the woman as a prissy creature becomes clear. Lawrence says:

There are the women who are cocksure, and the women who are Hensure. A really up-to date women is a cocksure women she doesn't have a doubt not a qualm. She is the modern type. Whereas the old fashioned demure woman was sure as a hen is sure, that is, without knowing about it she went quietly and busily clucking around, laying the eggs and mothering the chickens in a kind of anxious dreams that still was full of sureness, but not mental sureness. Her sureness was a physical condition, very soothing, but a condition out of which she could be startled or frightened. *(Scholes, Robert et al 2004:10)*

Robin S. Ngangom, while joining hands with Lawrence in preventing the rudiments of the feminine psychology, does not become contented with the sloppy practice of the women. The inherent potential of a women, which can even assume devastative dimensions, are never merely glanced at, rather he ponders over the twist that can happen in the world regarding the male and female roles and which can alter the very course of history where the male may be placed in front of the female with extended and upturned arms, begging the munificence of the female. Here the tenderness of a women which mostly interpreted as weakness of a female, gradually fades and she is predisposed to accumulate elements of rage and here her identity fuses with that of Durga, the Goddess of Indian mythology. This unpredictable transition, through which the woman assuming a very coveted positions in the patriarchal social system is presented, in the poem "To a woman from Southeastern Hill." Here Robin S. Ngangom says:

Will you woman, devastate these dreams
As men ravage the hills, leaving only
Scars and litter behind, after all hopes
Have been mind? Woman from the land
Of chhura, our roots suck from the
Same liquid tongue . Because of these
Shared dreams and waters, none knows you
Like I do; I who can nurture the twin syllables
Of your name. Speak again woman,
With your dulcet tongue, for this is the desire
Of these hills and yearning stores (*TDOR: 20)*

The ivy-like existence of a woman, gradually dries up in the scorching patriarchal glace, which in the disguise of providing an abundant supply of the requirements for proper growth, really becomes instrumental of in its total extinction. The capricious temperamental states of the male, often forcefully demand from the part of a female, mainly of the identity is one of 'wife', greater care regarding her own emotional states where the boiling or outbursting emotions are never tolerated by the society as woman, is brought purposefully, under the category of the icons of patience. Here she is evacuated from the rough zones of character deformities, but of course not for glorification rather patriarchy finds even here, possibilities of wringing out the individually from her for a larger exploitation through which his supremacy can again be made conspicuous. Even the gesticulations of a woman also come under the purview of patriarchy to place woman under a commonly agreed denomination, in order to deplete the freedom of a woman so that the process of 'mechanization' may be more readily accessible to the male. The excruciating agony suffered by a woman and the inescapable bond of a woman to the household, which at times becomes bondage, where on many occasions, she is forced to were the garment of a 'doltish being' and how even amidst all these a woman survives, is a question of relevant and through the poem "Weekend", Robin S. Ngangom makes a brushwork of such an enduring woman:

> .... The man starts berating, then beating the woman
> Rather slowly, not violently
> As if he is scrubbing a costly vase
> Afraid to break her
> The woman bowls in the still, humid nights
> ...... In the morning the man teases the woman in bed
> The woman not angrily, but rather pleasantly says
> Please stop this not in front of the children
> They share a smoke. After a while the woman
> Gets up. She goes to the kitchen and sings
> A popular film song (*WATS: 34)*

Here we get a typical picture an Indian women along with the carousing male in the Indian context where nobody empathizes with her, rather emotive, sympathetic words flood her vicinity of suffering, which instead of providing a consolation pricks her deep down in the heart bringing to the realm of her memory visions of a homely existence. Robin S. Ngangom, being a mosaic writer, gathers the little pebbles of female life to erect a mansion which would certainly delineate a 'complete woman' with all her frailities, frustrations, powers and potentials. In the modern life a woman feels, in an irreparable way zonked due to the diverse pressures that trounce her and brings herself esteem down to the lowest pedestal and even while she is numb, due to the diverse factors she is made liable to carry out the different roles which no one except her could execute with perfection. These lifelong enterprises of a woman, beginning initially as a daughter and passing through 'woman' 'wife' and 'mother' and of course a laudable enterprise get portrayed in "A poem for Mother." Here the poet expressed his thorough awareness regarding a woman especially a mother:

> I know how you toil as all mothers do
> For unmarried sons and aging husband
> And aberated daughters in - law
> Worried about us, for a long time
> Your lips couldn't blossom into a smile
> Times have furrowed your dear face and
> The first signs of snow are on your hair (*WATS: 24)*

Unlike a man, a woman has the capacity to be there in the extremes as her nature is a highly flexible one. She can be grave and pure, as the demand of the circumstances and these incredible dimensions of the nature make her completely stay beyond the grasp of the male, who can understand her only in biological terms. A woman can even scrimp and allocate what is gathered out of it for higher purposes. This positive life enduring tendency largely found among the poor, banished one of the countryside who can placate themselves with their little joys and hopes, gets a representation in the poem "Imphal" and here too, Robin S. Ngangom points an accusing finger at the incompatible behavioural patterns of the male in his treatment of the female, where he becomes a demi-god and the female a subject carry out anything and everything for the male. Here he says:

.... The mained woman with meager leaves
In the bazaars imploring pity
The men loading over them
And the girls ubiquitous
Spying from balconies
On display with renovated faces
In streets, in colleges,
Girls context as beauty queens. *(TC: 62)*

Robin S. Ngangom, like many other poets, exercises his poetic skills in pursuit of the sinuous, serpentine beauty of nature and in this attempt, often contrary to his sturdy confidence he finds the incongruity that has befallen the state of affairs in the present due to the impact of the past. The obnoxious appearance of the man and material in the present day, brought about mainly as a result of the flowering of the natural culture, nauseates the poet, but even here in this sorry state of nature too he, obviously perceive the dramatic female life, shows of its plumy magnificence which is projected out by the male in the open social scenario. The masquerade conducted by the male in his approach to the female mostly guided not by love but by lust comes under sharp criticism in the hands of Robin S. Ngangom in the poem "When You Do Not Return" and here he invites the attention of the public to the parallel transitions occurring in the life of a woman as well as in nature both of which are prey to the noxious consumerist culture of the male. The poet discovers:

Leaves no longer respond
To the alchemy of seasons
And the heart lies fallow
Expecting winter rain. Erath
Has closed again like a woman
When you do not return and dreams
Turn to rust, the flame and the dew
Cannot create art. Only lust breaks
On the branches of night, and men
Wear hideous marks, the fragrance
Of the wild rose is lost, and only
The flowers of the market are on sale. *(TDOR: 59)*

Robin S. Ngangom, as inveterate spokesperson for the feminine cause, does not completely denounce the male or his contributions to the ornamentation of the earth, may be through a process of scaffolding provided to the female, by which he expects to bring about a rare Socialism in the uniform endeavours and existence of the male and the female- these he expects to uplift the woman form the dungeons, of infamy into which she is cast from time immemorial as a result of the implementation of the rotten social codes, which no longer bears any worth or value today. Robin S. Ngangom, through experiences, have come to the broader generalizations, that earth appeals to be uncomfortable and inadequate to a jittery female, because only the one with a fighting spirit amidst the travails of the day could more forward with firm steps. He is expectant of the ultimate crowning of the female along with the male when he will never have to lament as he did in "Arms will flower here too." (*TC : 52)* The poet's intention is not to bring to light, what the revolutionaries want but to highlight, the unheard cries of the innocent women and children, who are left unnoticed many a time. Robin. S. Ngangom gains momentum in his poems because of the feministic values he regards. Boldly he asserts the doormat status of a woman and can identify himself with the pain in her. In "Weekend":

> The man comes home drunk
>
> He bangs at the door,
>
> Shouting at the woman
>
> Bleary-eyed the woman opens the door....
>
> The woman cleans up
>
> After a while all is silence (*WATS: 34)*

The picture is a candid representation of many a homes, and the female status of being trampled upon mercilessly. In "There is a consummate Woman", the poet beautifies the physical and mental aspects of a woman:

> Her steps are light
>
> Untouching the stones of the street.
>
> Her body bamboo-supple....
>
> Her laughter possesses my soul
>
> ...... I will wait
>
> For her to walk all over my life (*WATS: 54)*

3. Conclusion

The strength of Robin S. Ngangom's work is in the fact that he does not criticize but empathizes - his strong sense of belonging, enables him to empathize with people whom he has never seen, but know are his own. The poet cannot afford to waste his precious time on jeremiads. Many of his poems reflect a heart that yearns to understand and to be understood. His poetry springs from his own experiences or from the events he has absorbed, into the core of his being and felt so deeply that they fill his heart and poetry flows from it. The frequently recurring and dominant themes in the poetry of Robin S. Ngangom are linked to Socialism and Feminism in the same way as sea is linked to water or atmosphere to air. Immense love for the home state, pity for the pathetic situation of his people, empathy for the down trodden, the misled, the poor and the second sex are the chief underlying emotions of his poetry. His poetry gives the impression to the reader, that here is a poet who's real self and ideal self are identical, that here is a poet who romances with Socialism and Feminism without any prior concern. He deals with Socialism because he loves people, and with Feminism because he realizes that gender discrimination exists and women are the objects.

The central theme in the poetry of Ngangom is the all pervading love which is not only physical but spiritual. The innate tendency in most of the living organisms is to love and to be loved. When people begin to take weapons in the false hope of bringing peace to the nations the poet cannot keep mum living and loving have clearly become endangered aspirations. But in the face of that daily siege, the ability of Ngangom's poetry to 'sing' seems to have stayed intact. The ideas arising in the conscious self of the poet are transmitted into not only the head but also the hearts of the readers (for his poetry digs into the intellectual and the emotional appeal) in a way that they gestate in the mind of the reader. The poetry of Robin S. Ngangom has a universal appeal. His verses have the magical power to bring minds together and at the same time to hold them apart. Everyone gets the message that the writer wants to convey and at the same time there is sufficient scope for anyone to draw out his own conclusions. He never intends to convey a message rather invites the reader to draw a message from his verses. He exhibits an unusual fascination for truth and beauty. He shows abundant courage to be critical of those he loves. His diction has a texture that the reader can neither forget nor describe. The picturesque quality of his verses is praiseworthy.

Robin S. Ngangom in his poems justifies his stand as a socialist and a feminist, believing that a writer does not need a tradition to lean upon, but can be influenced by anything. The poet is a sociologist shows his increasing concern and his poetry is a form of social progress. He believes that all people should be viewed as moral equals, which entails, an anti-oppression liberationist philosophy, toward all people. Furthermore the poet believes that, literature is one of the official natures, touching upon the rights of women that fosters, protects and expresses that dignity in the exercise of freedom, is necessary. Any individual can make difference to a society. Robin S. Ngangom is one of these individuals who, makes his mark through poetry inspired by a hill-world. "If I had not made use of this hill-world, my poetry would have been false".

6
Conclusion

1. Romance

"Romance" is a type of narrative, nearest of all literary forms to the wish-fulfillment dreams. When thought of as a literary genre with romantic love or highly imaginative unrealistic episodes forming the central theme, romance refers to a style of heroic prose and verse that was visible in a fastidious manner in the aristocratic literature of medieval and early modern Europe, that dealt with extravagantly fanciful stories about the astonishing adventures of a chivalrous protagonist, often of supernatural ability, who goes on a quest. During the Medieval and early modern era the romance writers focused more on the adventures the protagonist come across and less on love and sentiment. They were built upon the legends and fairy tales to supply their characters with marvelous powers. The Romance is distinguished from the epic representing not a heroic age of tribal wars, but a courtly and chivalric age often one of highly developed manners and civility. Unlike the supernatural in epics, Romance shifted the supernatural to this world making much of the mysterious effect of magic, spells and achievements. Romance also celebrated rustic life, against a backdrop of Mother Nature. Romances were at first written in verse, but later in prose as well. Romance has been a staple of popular literature from the time of Greek romances (second and third centuries A.D) till date.

"Romance" originally, signified a written work in the French language, which evolved from a dialect of the Roman language, Latin. The romance literature that was written in old French and Anglo-Norman, was later imitated in English beginning with "Beowulf" (www.alcyone.com/max/lit/beowulf/) and August Wilhelm Schlegel, the renowned German thinker whose original work consisted mainly of poems, especially sonnets *Gedichte (1800)*. Chrétien de Troyes was one of the most distinguished French composers, who showed remarkable skills in combining the love story with the adventure story. Some of his notable poems are, *Erec (1170), Cligès (1176), Yvain* and *Lancelot (both written simultaneously between 1177 and 1181)* and *Perceval* (*written between 1181 and 1190, but left unfinished)*. Three, 13th century German poets produced one notable romance each: Hartman von *Aue's Iwein (1203)*; Gottfried von Strassburg *Tristan und isult (1210)*; and Wolfram von Eschenbach *Parzifal (1210)*.

Most of the romances during the late 12th century and 13th century were written in prose. They may be classified as follows according to subject:

(a) The first and foremost romance was of *King Arthur*. Geoffrey of Monmouth began it in England about 1132. Some of the main romances connected with the Arthur legend are *Arthur and Merlin, Morte d' Arthur, Sir Gawain and the Green knight* and *Sir Tristerm*.

(b) The second romantic story was that of *Charlemagne and His Twelve Peers*. Begun in France with the *Song of Roland*, a huge tale of Charlemagne was forged about 1110 in the name of Archbishop of Turpin. The popular romances of Charlemagne theme were *Otinel, The Roland, The Charlemagne and Roland, Siege of Milan, Sir Ferumbras,* and the humorous *Rauf Coilyear*.

(c) The third romantic story is that of the *Life of*

Alexander. King Alisaunter and *The Destruction of Troy* belong to this category.

(d) Various romances deal with miscellaneous themes. *King Horn, Havelock the Dane, Guy of Warwik* and *Bevis of Hampton* deal with English history. *William of Palerne* is written on the familiar "missing heir" theme. *Floris and Blauchefleur* depict the love of a king's son for a captive maid. *(S. Kumar. 2005: p. 9.)*

It was towards the end of the 13th century that themes of courtly love, such as faithfulness in adversity were emphasized in Romance literature. England produced two great romances in the 14th century; the popular *Lay of Havelok the Dane (1280 -1290)* and the aristocratic romance of *Sir Gawain and the Green Knight (late 14th century).* The traditions and codes of romance remained evident during the Renaissance period, in the poems of Ariosto and Tasso, in Spencer's *Faerie Queene (1590-1596)* and in numerous other works.

Romance is associated with the two greatest names of Renaissance literature, Shakespeare and Cervantes. Shakespeare's contribution lies in his plays, *Cymbeline (1609), The Winter's Tale (1610),* and *The Tempest (1613).* All these plays employ events, coincidences and episodic structure central to the romance form. Cervantes moved from the traditional romance into a new dimension, by suggesting a connection between the ideals of romance and the brutal facts of reality. His commitment to the world of romance is the subject of ridicule and satire, but at the same time the imaginative ideal exists. Cervantes' masterpiece, *Don Quixote (1605-15)* had a considerable influence on the picaresque narrative of adventure and on the novel in general, during the 19th century. Beaumont's comedy *The Knight of the Burning Pestle (1607)* may well have been influenced by Cervantes; Samuel Butler modeled his splendid mock-heroic poem *Hudibras (1663,64,78)* on

Don Quixote; and in the following century, Fielding described his novel *Joseph Andrews (1742)* as an imitation Cervantes' masterpiece.

In the 19th century, three very different novelists wrote a large number of works which can be variously classified as kinds of romance. They were, Sir Walter Scott, Nathaniel Hawthorne and George Meredith. Most of Scott's historical novels had their roots in the kind of material of which, older forms of romance were composed, but Scott's approach were realist and he sought to make his characters permanent. Hawthorne and Meredith set their romance in the contemporary scene. Hawthorne's more notable works are *The House of the Seven Gables (1851)* and *The Marble Faun (1860).* A good representative example of the kind of romance Meredith wrote is *The adventure of Henry Richmond (1871).* The term Romance, had become a capacious category embracing the majority of fiction, drama, and poetry. According to Nathaniel Hawthorne,

> When a writer calls his work a Romance... he wishes to proclaim a certain latitude." (*1851: 1)*

The concept of Romance underwent a further modification, at turn of the 18th century, the era called 'The Romantic Age' or the revival of 'Romanticism'. The term 'Romance' meant something that could happen, a new conception that romance was a revitalizing force. Romanticism revived the romance in verse form.

Romanticism does not have much to do with things popularly thought of as "romantic" although love, occasionally may be the subject of romantic art and literature. Romanticism can be considered as an international artistic and philosophical movement that redefined the fundamental voice in which people in western cultures, thought about themselves and about their world. It is an astonishing fact that the strongholds of the Romantic Movement were England and Germany and not countries which are known for romance languages. Romanticism is said to have begun in the year 1798, the year of the first edition of *Lyrical Ballads* by Wordsworth and Coleridge. However it is generally accepted that as an international movement, affecting all the arts, Romanticism began at least in the 1770's and continued into the second half of the 19th century. Romanticism originated in an age of revolutions. The American Revolution (1776) and the French Revolution (1789) coincide with the early romantic period. A revolutionary energy was also at the core of Romanticism, which quite consciously set out to transform, not only the theory and practice of poetry but the very way we perceive the world. It should be noted that the revolutionary energy underlying the Romantic Movement affected not only literature but all of the arts – from music to painting, and sculpture to architecture.

Romanticism has been variously defined. Romanticism is liberalism in literature. According to W.J. Long, "The essence of Romanticism was that literature must reflect all that is spontaneous and unaffected in nature and in man, and be free to follow its on fancy and its own way" *(1989: 372)*. Romanticism was hoisted with full flaps by French philosophers Voltaire, Diderot and Rousseau, who exposed the hollowness of the European social system, stressing upon 'noble savage' and the democratic ideals of Liberty, Equality and Fraternity. 'A return to Nature' in all its glorious aspects and thereby, a regeneration of mankind was the conscious and unconscious work of the Romantic Writers. Romanticism was a humanitarian philosophy for society. Imagination, nature, symbolism and myth were given great prominence in the Romantic conception of art. As far as Romanticism was concerned symbols were the human aesthetic correlatives, of nature's emblematic language. The Romantics were ambivalent toward the real social world around them. They were often politically and socially involved, but at the same time began to distance themselves from the public. High romantic artists interpreted things through their own emotions, and these emotions included social and political consciousness, as one would expect in a period of revolution. The Romantics reacted strongly to oppression and injustice in the world; they created an atmosphere of instability and at times, turbulence. Through their poetry, the poets gave a message to the entire human race- To live, to love and build a just and peaceful society.

As a literary movement Romanticism has ended, but off and on the romantic elements are found in the contemporary literature. The salient features of the Romance literature have continued into the modern age with the same vigor it had in the beginning, but with a different orientation. The essence of Romanticism was that literature must reflect all that is spontaneous and unaffected in nature and in man and be free to follow its own way, thereby a regeneration of mankind. As Samuel Taylor Coleridge writes,

> If poetry instructs, it does so only through pleasure.
> *(Scott. 1946.p.48.)*

In other words, Romanticism was humanitarian philosophy for society. This humanitarian philosophy has been romanced in the social and feminist context by poets of Indo-Anglian literature. The fact that, elements of Romanticism was visible in the Indian poetry, though not as a movement, remains as an unquestionable truth. For many of the great Indian poets, poetry was akin to a form of meditation. Spirituality lies at the heart of the Vedic poetry, which was written in a language that was more musical than any existing language. As in every other sphere of life poetry too was not rigid in India, it accepted changes as and when they embraced literature just like it did in social life. In England Romantic poetry was dependent on a number of features that were peculiar to the time of its origin: Many of the Romantic poets used it as a weapon against previous literary styles. Romantic poetry was used in those days, to question the teachings of philosophers who were admired till then. The created gained predominance over the creator in many of the romantic poems.

Though India was politically in upheavals, at the time of the rise of Romanticism, it is difficult to attribute the various features of Romantic poetry in England to the Romantic Movement in India. The Indian culture, highly centered, not on a far-fetched but closer reality, had ever in its magical casket of unsophisticated beauty, the wonders of charm and elegance, deriving from the ethical and moral dimensions as well as the natural and stark realities, of day to day life. In the presentation of such a wonderful and magnificent reality, the role played by the poet can never be sidelined as they, having a convergence of diverse streams of thought-related to melancholy, happiness, sterility, segregation, separation, indifference etc. in the form of poetic expressions, have been superimposed with the Herculean task of the expression of the hitherto unexplored emotional outbursts. In this context, the Romantic poets do play a vital role of their own. Romanticism, as is often thought, does not merely talk about the buntings on human life, rather it is a manifestation, often of the nail-biting, hair-raising experiences of life that have the added flavor of the real reflection of the actualities of everyday life.

The Indian poetry, as it is an offshoot or an extension of the Indian tradition and cultural characteristics, amply includes, within its scope the liking for the 'country culture' or the 'culture of the nature' which itself has formed part of the greatest element of romanticism. The traditional Indian culture as if in a mirror, in the Indian poetry where the lives of the humans merge with that of the elements and the elemental forces. Toru Dutt was a writer, who could even portray the tragic dimension of Romanticism. The 'hide and seek' of destiny unveils itself in the poetry of Toru Dutt. Even the very frame of a Causarina tree, of course part of the, greatest romantic element nature, adorned by the climbing creepers could bring to her mind not only the beauty of nature, but also the existential dilemma of the human beings. It even embarks on a theme of death, yet another major preoccupation of the romantic writers.

The anguish and anxiety of a village woman in the poetry of Sarojini Naidu, develops itself in to a conglomeration of diverse life, centered queries that express the repercussions and retaliations of the evils, larking behind the multifaceted social scenario. This aspiration, to be part of the greatest force, sharing the dejections, disappointments and the remarkable rendezvous, where the synthesis of the existential with the existing and the eternal occur, is revealed before the very eyes of the readers in the poetry of Sarojini Naidu. The halo of a crystal clear romantic temperament is found in her poem "Ecstacy":

Cover mine eyes, oh my love
My eyes that are weary of bliss
As of light that is poignant and strong
Oh silence my lips with a kiss
My lips that are weary of songs.

Here the poet makes all the romantic elements, the instrument to carry the innate emotional ingredients, where element of love finds a fusion with that of, the artistic talent of spontaneity in expression. The poet never severing herself from the periphery of the romantic world expresses the inborn feelings, with subtlety of one having personal experience with the truest and staunchest aspects of life, that are determined to the smooth running in the course of human life. Even A.K. Ramanujan is a poet who could visualize the tragic beauty of Romanticism in the flooding river. When death became a matter for celebration, there Romanticism assumes another dimension, projecting out the beauty of 'ugliness'.

The poems of Parthasarathy too, very vividly portray the Romantic elements, though in a grim and melancholic aspect. The vast plethora of experiences that are both life generating and life negating makes the poet to perceive the world in different ways, where even the interiors of the 'Warehouse' has a never ending story to tell which may be the saddest of the stories ever told. He is a poet who could even see the glimpse of Romanticism in poetry, where the underdogs and the downtrodden though living in the verge of a threat of extinction, they maintain the 'self' which never comes under the purview of degeneration. This upright attitude, though not visible in the body, makes even a fisherman with tattered and torn nets to maintain the perseverance and self-preservation.

Thus in Indian English poetry, there are ample evidences to the manifestation of Romanticism, though it is markedly a deviation from the British Romanticism. In the Indian context, the tones and mood of the romantic element is tinged, more with the stark realities and the subsequent apathies. The metamorphosis experienced by each individual in diverse contexts gets itself completely unmasked to include all the dimensions of life which are both happy and sad. Indian English poetry is rich in romantic elements, surpassing even the parental branch of the British Romanticism.

The literature of North-East India has also taken on the Romantic humanitarian philosophy, and the poets of the region, are a touchstone, judging and evaluating everything on earth, as far as the eye could see. North-East India cannot wait anymore for slow plans. It is only a crash course that can save the day. Temsula Ao, Monalisa Changkija and Robin S. Ngangom differ from the other contemporary writers in a significant way. What is common to these three writers is the overwhelming love for the battered and the socially stratified in their works. They live with the menace of corruption, terror and the guns, which paints their poetry. Most of their poems researched, expose a society that is under moral and social threat. The quest for truth, liberty and harmony are the underlying passions in most of these poems. The silent bloodless revolution intended by the poets is of the same intensity. The infringement of the law and order, in the name of any kind of reason is regretted by the poets. Furthermore, Feminism has been tiptoed on. Women produce children, women are mothers and wives, women do the cooking, mending, sewing, and washing, they take care of men, and are subordinate to male authority, they are largely excluded from high status occupations and from positions of power. These generalizations apply to some degree, to practically every known human society. The three writers under study, strongly revolt against these long held assumptions. The institution of marriage has been instrumental, in the fall of many a woman into the hands of men, who finds practically no difference between a wife and a domestic animal. This attitude of the andocentric society is severely criticized in the poetic works of these writers. In today's world where a person's worth is determined by what he can buy, Temsula Ao, Monalisa Changkija and Robin S. Ngangom stand apart. The three poets are a tolerant lover of people and devoted protagonists of peace. The poems of Temsula Ao, Monalisa Changkija, and Robin S. Ngangom are relevant to the times of the North-East Region and the poets have assumed a stand to touch the burning issues of Socialism and Feminism.

Temsula Ao has been the most prolific poet of the North-East India. Lyricism, verbal melody, economy of expression and mellifluous language, and the expression of stark realities of life make her poetry creditable. In the modern social discourses, which is highly oriented towards the feminine sensibilities, cultural deformations and strategic developments brought about as a result of temporarily tangible prosperity regarding a future, play a vital role in the rearrangement and reconstruction of the life of each individuals. The authority of social and cultural history, that is closely allied to the life and participating functions of the female, who is forced to form incrustations of isolation evolving out of the injected inferiority ,gets questioned in the modern era, due to the social tendency to dismantle the female and the 'Feminism' from the visible social scenario. The queasiness and the suffocation that each woman is made to undergo in the social sphere of her existence gradually makes her to move on to the mould of a shale, which is in outward appearance beautiful and protective but in reality something prone to easy transformations, even to the level of a breaking up. The diplomatic caliber of a female, whether it is in the social or familial context, could weld many a broken threads in these specific areas and often the beneficiaries of such settlements, mainly constituted of the male, fail to acknowledge the social value of those endeavors. The efforts made by any female to get out of the socially constructed shackles, which is a downright negation of any possibilities of Socialism, have been sty mired by the arrogant male ego preaching a lot but practicing nothing. Temsula Ao's poetry in this respect is an attempt to assert a sturdy Socialism even in the feminine cause, through which alone, could one dream of the advent of the perfection of Socialism.

Temsula Ao's poetry keeps itself aloof, from the hullabaloo to look at reality with a saddened face to make one lament, on the gradual transition of humanity especially that of the female in to the state of 'rigor mortis' due to the oppressive measures with which she has been inflicted for ages. The parting that has befallen the humanity, manifesting itself in the form of diverse degradations occurring in multiple spheres of everyday life, deprives him of everything that was once, part and parcel of him and it sojourns him to an imaginary, unrealistic world where the horrible and the horrifying nightmarish occurrences haunts his life to install a catastrophic finale to his life. Temsula Ao looks at these cotemporary realities from the view point of a poet, to draw a parallel with the evergreen days of the past when the paralysis of the day had not even opened up, the first symptoms of a disaster. According to Temsula Ao, today everyone plays the role of a twerp in the eyes of the other, as the contemporary man has lost the harmonious 'collectivist' mentality, which was the visible vestige of a prosperous past's Socialism and today the term 'personal' has gained more currency, over the term 'social' so that the togas of hypocrisy and the resultant selfishness form part of the day to day garment of the individual. Temsula Ao is melancholic to note the loss of fluency in the 'emotional lexicon' especially in man-woman relationship and she advocates the philosophy of a Socialism, even here to ensure a confluence of the male and the female, through, which alone, according to her the discomfort of the modern era could be revoked.

Temsula Ao's poetry, by advocating the larger dimensions of Socialism in all fields of life, especially in the wintry existence of the male and the female, aims at the installation of a rollicking social situation through which the cultural as well as the social antithesis can be rewritten, to assume a kind of concurrence with that of the demands made by the travails of the day, which if not remedied at the earliest, would witness the slipstream of disasters and that may spell the doom of a generation. The gigantic posture of the male over the female, with which he imposes the Herculean tasks on the female, comes under the scrutinizing eyes of Temsula Ao, as she enters deep down into the male and female psyche to pluck out the basic roots of the discord existing in the strained relationship of the once conjoined pair and which was supposed to be an everlasting one until the doomsday. Temsula Ao is against the double standards of the society, strongly because the female is denied the chance of a choice. Every female ultimately finds an open treatment in the hands of Temsula Ao. Here rather than assuming the role of a severe critic, Temsula Ao subtly opens up before the readers a world of degenerated and degraded values, where it is shorn off its glory to appear in a very dull and dusky form, and through which, by focusing the attention of a generation on this specific social reality, aspects to bring about revisions in the code of conduct of the society, which may propel the society to rise above the existing disorderliness.

Temsula Ao's poetry, while perceived in the background of the socio-political conflicts of the specific geographical region of the North-East, has the abundance of emotional fevour associated with it as it has the musicality and the rhythm of the throbbing hearts of a sect of people who have undergone the scurrilous antipathy from many sources. Temsula Ao speaks so the situation in the poem "My Substance" where she expects to have a cathartic effect through the spoken poetic words:

I had once
Yearned for home
But on reaching
Found only walls
Walls
Empty words
Illusive rainbows
My substance
All *(STT : 58.)*

When one glances through the poetry of Temsula Ao , we find a series of unfulfilled yearnings which presented as that of the poet in its regional or universal appreciation speeds of the ever suppressed dreams of a sect of people or that of the entire humanity, but the figure who, with the unquenchable thirst for rejuvenation from the contemporary schemes working within the society, rises above ordinary human beings in the poetry of Temsula Ao is the female who has been bestowed with the scepter of the glorified motherliness to place her on the last pedestal of social life. Temsula Ao's poetry, in a pacy rhythm, reveals the vibrancy of a group that has been largely suppressed due to diverse causes and tries to ignite the hearts of both the victor and looser, the suppresser and the suppressed, the male and female, with a view to establish the social order which will cease to be a jerky Socialism, rather one founded on the edifice of pliable social and personal relationships.

Temsula Ao, as a recorder of the socio-cultural life of a region ,along with the anguish caused by the socio-political developments of the day, deals in detail with risible aura provided to a woman by the patriarchal society through which she is perpetually made of oscillate between her 'real self' – with all the sense, sensations and sensibilities of a woman – and the 'assumed self'- that which she develops as a result of the entanglement in the intricate nexus of responsibilities and demands made by the society. Here, Temsula Ao finds the catastrophic of the feminine world transferring itself into the form of a mush of 'feminine desires' and masculine demands ' in which the woman is destined to pawn her 'self ' before the patriarchy. Thus the poetry of Temsula Ao read as essentially socialistic and feminine proclaims a Socialism in Feminism through which the patriarchal norms that have been brandished at the female could be transformed into the patting hands of consolation.

Monalisa Changkija, in her poetry has portrayed social problems wondering if advancing into the new century is to be taken literally. Her poems, in a unique rhythm, stress individual and collective aspirations and ambitions, and the need to repent independence of spirit. Her poems are a personification of free will, blessed to human beings, which is a great gift. It is with legitimate praise and satisfaction that a reader completes even a brief and substantial piece of poetry of Monalisa Changkija, that speaks of the manifold activities, anxieties, doubts and deviations of a generation that savour, the joys and pleasure of everyday life even amidst the never to be sidelined pangs of the day. Bustling with enthusiasm, energy, creativity and dynamism is the modern generation especially the youth of the day. To orient this creative force for social reconstruction and reprogramming is an effort that requires great vision and for this the benevolent guidance is being provided by Monalisa Changkija through her poetry.

The innovative ideas opening its flood gates before the modern era, imbibing the motto of 'rejuvenation', capture the heart of each individual to sweep him aside into a sphere of 'creative genesis'. The commencement of a series of theoretical outbreak in the public social sphere of the day demanded higher commitments from the parts of the poets who, never losing a footing on the old can merge the present with the so called traditional and often the most cherished one, and for that which is not an easily attainable endeavour, the poets labour meticulously. Here the role of Monalisa Changkija as a poet of social concern is highly praiseworthy as she deals with the social issues through advocating the advent of Socialism. Often the tragic and highly lamentable events take place in the once prosperous social life which may be germinating out of the greedy lot who are concerned not of the outrageous nature of their activities. The exorbitant demands made by the contemporary social situations, mainly in the form of a transition from the old modes of life where one's role gets defined in the concrete terms of an iconoclast, shuns the very concept of a personal, individual dignity and worth where the personality of one get shattered and fragmented in the pellucid and extreme pull of social existence.

A radical departure from the traditional, especially in the case of a woman, tends to be seen with a frowning face where the conceptualized female figure, according to those who perceive it a transgression, trespasses into the iron-walled world of the male, which for them, is something that can never be tolerate as it possess a threat to the integrity of the hitherto unquestioned patriarchal world. The unethical speculations and gambling that places a woman in the tunnel of sufferings where she is made to sub-serve, the 'patriarchal aims' to achieve the growth and crowning of the male ego, that never comes across the hazards of prohibitions gets questioned on the poetry of Monalisa

Changkija. While a poet like Monalisa Changkija, who, sharing the sensibility of the female looked with a crucial eye at the nefarious practices of the patriarchy to suppress the female, many of the patriarchal circles viewed it as an utopian dream, of the poet to nib the fount of the patriarchal power. Yet Monalisa Changkija chalks out a series of plans for uplifting the female in the contemporary society, which neither attempts nor permits the enhancement of the feminine spirit and personality; but which would provide her the safety. Monalisa Changkija's poetry is an attempt to address these issues by understanding the influencing external and internal risk factors which may be media, social and cultural influences, race, gender segregation psychic turbulences, stress and poor coping skills of the female due to the pressure exerted on her. Here, according to Monalisa Changkija womanhood has been given another definition in the present day, radically divergent in nature from that of the traditional view points and it has become a period of problems, and frustrations devoid of romance and creativity and the individual within the body is without adequate freedom to express itself freely due to the oppressive measures adopted by the male; thus casting her completely into the twilight of existence, where she like a flickering flame waves in the slightest of antagonism in the poem "Of people unanswered - III" we hear the penetrating voice of the poet, addressing the cause of a generation, but through which one can even listen: if he stays close to the psychological realm of the poet sharing the feminine spirit and sensibility, the angered voice of a woman reacting against the mélange of norms that confines her in a poky world. The poet says:

Don't waste your time
Laying down diktats
And guidelines
On how to conduct my life
On matters personal and political
You may not know

Hey and the AK-47
And so you survive
Prosper in darkness
But I am more
Than a mere machine
Or a mass of molecules *(MM: 31)*

According to Monalisa Changkija, who dreams of the 'fraternity' and confluence of the male and the female world, the vulnerable nature of the female world brought about by the social or environmental factors that have an apocalyptic impact on the female life, does not merely affect the integrity of the female world, rather it raises severe questions of existential dilemma for the male world, as well as the social structure at large. The stressful experiences, of irritability inability to relax, restlessness, feeling of depression etc. becomes an appendage to the physical or biological experiences of a female. These diverse experiences can develop symptoms, of repeated reliving of experiences of the disasters that occurred in their life, a sense of numbness, and emotional blunting, detachment from others not responding to the circumstances and even the inability to respond and react to pleasant situations and avoiding all that which reminds her of the panicky past. Through her poetry Monalisa Changkija, like a firmly rooted psychoanalyst, unearths the pangs of the female to invite the attention of the public for the establishment of the Socialism, which may be a stalwart remedy to the degeneration of the contemporary world. Monalisa Changkija is a poet, having a great social awareness never lagging behind the historical developments and progress, where she realizes that the course of history is spotted with innumerable attempts to monopolize power ever since time immemorial.

Gender equality now becomes a subject that is raked up, dusted, displayed and finally abandoned once the media reports any major incident of discrimination or violence against women. After years of discussion and heated debates and arguments, it seems that it is set aside at least temporarily and the term itself - Feminism sounds like a false hope given to the deep rooted anti- female bias and the wide spread violation of woman's rights in the country. It is here, that Monalisa Changkija assuming the conspicuous poster and position of a feminist writer who has discovered, that the plight of women manifesting in different forms cannot be attributed to few causes alone, as it varies from cultural, social, economic to geographical and ecological factors. According to Monalisa Changkija even the mumbling of a women is pregnant with much more meaning, than it appease to carry and the reason why such a thing happens is due to suppression where opportunities are denied to her to air her viewpoints, so she has to get herself freed from the enslavement of introversion, an attributed quality to the traditional woman, to stand erect to face the patriarchal world with the boldness of the 'feminine psyche'.

Monalisa Changkija's poetry, is both passable and enjoyable. The poet envisions a world, where the possibility of a harmonious existence of the male and the female, is not far beyond the reach of the modern generation and where the 'hoi polloi', especially the woman, on the footing and pedestal of the socialist pattern, assume the dignity of an 'individual' freed from the clutches of all oppressive forces. Thus the poetry of Monalisa Changkija has the adequate credentials, to claim a feminist as well as socialist flavor of its own.

Robin S. Ngangom is a pioneering poet who has earned national and international repute. His poems, simple, easy, and lucid in diction, reflect all his feelings on social and feminist issues of the times. Social institutions, devised by human beings to coordinate the complicated and complex interactions of groups of human beings, as they exploit the bio-physical world and each other for their own advantage, often determines the course of life of a people in the increasing demands of the day, as to where or at what juncture of the historical progress could they attain and experience the verisimilitude of the entire reality of the era, which defies any kind of concrete and concentrated definitions. An analysis of social systems and institutions and the ways they are shaped by tradition, culture, history and political power, would reveal to the 'researching mind' the flamboyant patterns generated by these in the lives of a group of people, may be dwelling in the background of a specific geographical milieu.

The poems of Robin S. Ngangom excavate the internally cemented social discussions, in the day to day existence of an individual, when the 'power politics' material malpractices reign to jeopardize the simplicity of their daily existence. Here Robin S. Ngangom has been shaken awake to the stark reality, which is not merely a disturbing one, but a horrendous one, that shatters the self confidence of one to thin pieces, that people are not able to satisfy their psychological needs even while they race for the material progress and growth. He, as one sensitive to the individual inclinations, seeks alternative possibilities for the eradication of that legacy of perpetual gloom, resulting mainly from the western 'throw away' or 'disposable' culture which has disturbed the existing social framework in a very drastic manner. Robin S. Ngangom, through his poems points an accusing finger at the contemporary materialistic trends that have taken a very heavy toll in the form of a bankruptcy, may be in the emotional sphere, due to the desperate bid for recognition as 'modern' and the psychological and visual ecstasy that they may derive out of these, have not been realized as temporary, leading to the extinction of much that is beyond the assessment of worth. The ingenious people may be a minority, with their frenzy ideas come forward, with their promises of bestowing the latest benefits of the modern culture, due to which, according to Robin S. Ngangom yet, another history of men inflicting such emotional torture on themselves get written. Here distinction can never be made, regarding the male and the female as both stand at the receiving end of this historical reality and here, the concept of Socialism gradually fades into the misty world of avarice conflicts, where the quest of a woman, for self does not get a recognition.

As we go through the poems of Robin S. Ngangom, what opens before us is a world of the female in a glassy mode, and the Feminism that he advocates, is not a western oriented because it is born out of a typically Indian context from the infectious social situation, where the female is attracted to the maximum, that brings about an absence of concrete experiences and a situation of intellectual psychological and even sexual starvation. Robin S. Ngangom through his poetry, however, transcends those cultural times when sex was conspicuous by its non-mention and he focuses his attention on woman – her travails and privations, tensions and irritations, pains and anguishes and at the same time, he negates not the role played by women for their own victimization. It is only through analysis and self-understanding, through vigilance and average they can begin to change their lives and they will have fought their own battles.

Robin S. Ngangom's poems, while dealing with the feminist aspects; brings in the imagery of 'witness' frequently to suggest the feminine qualities in the most concrete forms. He has realized that, the Indian context is one of a pro-man situation, a negation of Socialism, where the attempts to curb the gruesome disparities existing in the treatment of the male and the female are very fragile and that it never assures the safeguarding of the female interests. According to him, though at the surface level it may seem that women have been empowered and are on par with men, there is in fact a well unintended prejudice against women, in the mindset of the society and only though the dissemination of the idea of gender justice could we place women along with men in horizons of glory.

Robin S. Ngangom, visualized the emergence of a new

social order supported by the cultural forces where the most range of human potential is spent to all irrespective of their caste, creed, religion or sex, and here he finds the socialist pattern of the society. As far as Robin S. Ngangom is concerned the gun shots and the whispers and wailing, resulting from them cannot be remedied through a schmaltzy piece of poetry and the situation as even more grave as one imagines it to become. The poem "The strange affairs of Robin S. Ngangom" brings out the gravity of the situation that has marked the lopsided social situation. Here within the brevity of a few lines, he reveals the feminine cause along with the very pathetic social situation:

> uprightness is not causing anything publicly,
> Integrity is not drinking
> Worthiness is contributing generously to a new faith
> to buy guns for unleashing ideological horror
> service is milking the state
> and when you can lift no more
> to start burgling each other
> so that we can become paragons of thievery
> chastity is forbidding our women
> from exposing thick legs
> purity is not whispering
> even a solitary world of love
> so that it will not be mistaken
> for unpardonable obscenity *(TDOR: 68)*

Attempts made by the antagonistic forces to obliterate the social order never escape the ever conscious eyes of Robin S. Ngangom. He makes his poetry a weapon, not to harm, but to resist and to redeem reacts to these demonic forces functioning as undercurrents in the social scenario, but he never resorts to the expletives even while being an eye witness to the savagery of the day. The decadence of the socio-political and even cultural aspects attracts the attention of the poet to investigate the plunder happening even in the personal lives of the people some, though not active participants in the potential problems of the day, are made to go plummeting down into the unfathomable crevices of disasters, distortions and the all consuming gluttony.

Today, according to Robin S. Ngangom, everywhere, what one perceives is the remorsefully bowed head of humanity, ashamed of its own ravages through the last glimmer of a harmonious social being was extinguished and the only anti-venom to this vital disease of the day is nothing but the establishment of the socialist order, where no more gun shots will be heard and that will gradually transfer the mourning visages from the frame of social life. Robin S. Ngangom is highly optimistic of the gradual disappearance of the truculent tendencies, that overshadows the contemporary society and that which demoralizes the social framework, any collective endeavor will, better the social situation. But even amidst these optimistic ideas, he is not without certain trepidations regarding the future of the female and Socialism while looking at the 'way of the world' that is moving from deformity to deformity and he is caught between this sorry reality and his inability to wean himself away from dreaming of a socialist pattern emerging and it is out of this choking situation that he says:

> I came looking for love
> and found only willows weeping here *(TC: 52)*

However, Robin S. Ngangom is a writer with a mission; to ensure the investiture of Socialism, through which the questions of feminine causes can also be adequately answered and reciprocated.

Place of Temsula Ao, Monalisa Changkija and Robin S. Ngangom

The poets of the North-East from various provinces

write on variety of themes. In general no two poets are similar in themes. But they have their own peculiar vision. Temsula Ao has bitter experience about the womanhood in Nagaland. But she is not very aggressive in exposing them like Monalisa Changkija or Lakshahira Das. She passively reveals the sufferings of women and her own sufferings. Reacting to her own obsession she says:

For twelve long miserable years
My life coursed away
At the core of my womanhood
Draining all joy and hope,
Tainting existence
With the leprous out-pouring
Of unhealing emanation *(STT: 37)*

Temsula Ao focuses on the man-woman cordial relationships. Her expression of bitter relationships is of a mild tone. In her poem entitled "Rites", she exposes the cordiality in divine terms:

Everytime we enact
The self-giving rite
I hold you deep within
The very best of you in
Primeval contact *(STTTS: 42)*

In her recent poems "Man to Woman" and "Woman to Man", she speaks of the Ao customs and traditions of marriage. In Ao tradition, before a man marries, he has to build a new house where he takes his wife to begin a new family *(2007:57)*. In the poem "Man to Woman", the bridegroom speaks to the bride the many reasons for which he has courted her. One of the reasons is given like this:

You may not be the prettiest
Nor the fairest of the village maidens

But when you smile
I see my world lit up in your face *(2007: 57)*

Against bitter patriarchal dominance, the feminist concerns of Temsula Ao reveal cordiality between the man and woman, which if implemented universally in the true sense of the term, will bring out a golden era, of humanist bond on socialist life. So Temsula Ao does not like to arouse controversy in revealing controversial relationships. On the other hand, she speaks of cordiality on the principle that "all is well that's begins/ends well." Similarly in the other poem "Woman to Man", the Ao bride, speaks to the bridegroom in fun honestly about the honest cordial relationship:

When you say I am not
The prettiest or the fairest
I am not angry
As I know I am no great beauty
I've also heard that you once
Snubbed a maiden, pretty but lazy
Saying, 'My sons' eyes
Will not fill their bellies.' *(2007: 60)*

These lives highlight true mutual understanding which is essential in conjugal life. By exposing this, Temsula Ao devises a new technique of Feminism. It means Feminism as a war/protest for equal rights may not bring peace. Peace can be maintained in peaceful bargain or reconciliation or perfect understanding. We do not find any other poet in North-East or other parts of India for comparison with Temsula Ao, because she is a different kind of visionary who never believes in war but believes in peace, with the conscience that peace can be achieved in peaceful way only.

Temsula Ao and Monalisa Changkija are both from

Nagaland, but thematically they are distinct and dissimilar. Monalisa Changkija is a social activist. She writes chiefly on the woman's suffering in Nagaland and the ecological depletion. Ecological changes due to industrialization, the hills changing shape and significance in modern times figure prominently in her poems. In this connection, she can be compared to Esther Syiem, a poet of Meghlaya. Esther, in her lone poetry collection, has narrated the folk tradition in Meghalaya. Though she never complained, against the ecological devastation in her homeland, she elaborates on the folk faiths and significance of the nature in her *Oral Scriptings (2005)*. She simply likes to narrate the legends available in Khasi Lore. But if we analyze the lore, we find that in those ancient days of animist faith, the tribal suffered due to their misdeeds or careless activities. In her poems "U Lum Sohpet Bneng" *(2005:pp.62-63)* and "Ka Jingkieng Ksiar" *(2005:pp.64-65)*, she narrates how the sixteen pristine Khasi families, who loved in heaven fell upon a bad time. Seven out of them came down to earth to settle. There was a golden ladder (Ka Jingkieng Ksiar) connecting the earth to heaven. The seven families in the earth out of ignorance cut down the ladder and thus the link, between the seven families on the earth and the nine in the heaven was cut off and the earth-and-heaven sacred relationship was disconnected. This is in legend and tells about the ecological inequilibrium, of the modern times which takes place due to the cutting of trees or deforestation and this phenomenon links to the idea of ecofeminism, in several of the poets of North-East like Kynpham Sing Nongkynrih, Easterine Iralu, R.K. Madhubir and others.

Monalisa Changkija is very aggressive about the perennial problems of Naga women, which Temsula Ao raises in her stories in *These Hills Called Home (2006)*. Temsula Ao narrates how Khatila saves the life of Punaba, her husband by telling lies to the army men and acting boldly bearing all atrocities. She suffered a lot during the absence of her husband in the house. The Naga women sacrificed a lot for their husbands and children and suffer all the odds in the way of life. But Monalisa Changkija, who raises basic questions about inequality, sexual discrimination and patriarchal domination, demands the equal rights for the woman. She is confident of the victory of the oppressed and has firm belief, that the oppressed will certainly win the wars in the conflict of power relations. She recurrently speaks of the maladies of women:

Dowryless Brides
Penny-less wives, and
Sonless mothers
Have their destinies written
On invisible
Tongues of flames *(WoWoPoP: 3)*

Like Monalisa, Lakshahira Das, a poet from Assam depicts the sufferings of women. Lakshahira reflects the predicaments of women in general and symbolizes male-domination as symbols of cruelty, selfishness and helplessness *(Das.2004:16)*. Lakshahira ambiguously highlights women "as pitiless as merchants, cruel as assassin" *(Das.1990:1)*. She depicts women's sorry state of life miserably:

Men are living up like ants
Bearing on their shoulders,
Ravished women
And naked forms of pallid children *(Das: 5)*

The oppressors of women have been punished severely. According to a Khasi legend, Manik Raitong, an orphaned youth, who had an illicit affair with the Syiem's wife had to face his sad death by the Syiem's order. U Manik Raitong, the wretched, is celebrated as the archetypal lover and the dispenser of the tradition of love and music in Khasi society *(Nongkynrih. 2007:129)*. Manik, in spite of his illicit affair, was an excellent musician, and before his immolation, he planted his bamboo flute which took root. Robin exploring this mysterious legend sings of the human predicament:

How sad is the lot of my friend Manik
Spelling his heart
From the seven mouths of his flute,
Even though he has dared to wear
The flower of the Syiem *(TC: 21)*

Similarly, Robin also speaks of a legendary lover couple of Manipur. A poor orphan of Moirang named Khuman Khamba loved the princess Thoibi. Their "love reached every lip of Moirang" *(WATS:28)* and the kind Chingkhu Naha Tellheiba and the crown prince Chingkhuba awarded capital punishment to Khamba. Here it is not the case of true love or else, but the virginity of the women and their status and holiness was honored in those olden days. When the poets retell these legends in their poetry, they highlight the honor of women and its disregard in our time. By that, they try to uphold the feminist principles. About Khamba and Khoibi, Robin hints:

Khamba the orphan, the tall silent one,
Khamba of the bamboo-groves
who possessed nothing
but the princess he loved *(WATS: 28)*

Robin explored the destinies of women throughout the history and with his radical socialist out-look he has questioned the integrity of women, which expose his ambivalent stand as to the feminist ideology:

I wanted to know women,
What lies beneath that mystical exterior,
But in this too I was defeated *(WATS: 52)*

Again he respects the greatness of women, when he says how sincerely he wants to explore their destinies:

I consecrate all my lines to her
And she just walks across them
She is the kind of being
I will search through myths of despair. *(WATS: 54)*

Robin touches upon a great variety of themes, being the most representative poet from North-East. He is both national and international in his themes. Because of the large circumference of his poetry, he is beyond comparison to any other poet of North-East and can only be compared, with Jayanta Mahapatra and the Latin American poets by whom, as he says, he has been influenced. This comparison lies in his choice of local themes and choosing images from indigenous landscapes which we find throughout his poetry.

As regards his romance with socialist outlook, it can be observed how at the failure of Socialism in Russia, prevalence of utter misery and poverty in Moscow, he breaks down and laments for the demolition of the great culture, art and poetry. He does prefer "democracy's gospel/ (that) has been heard in Russia's churches" *(TC:53)* and opines:

I wanted Russia to remain suffering
From the steppes to Siberia,
Looking for truth in its own breaking heart,
Not listening to the whispers of the west *(TC: 53)*

He protest against the death of Socialism with his own words "with the deafening heavy metal of the west/ be sung at Leningrad as improvised anthems" *(TC: 54)* and sorrowfully bemoans the death of the rich aesthetic traditions of Russia:

The west breaks out into beatific smiles
But how terrible that Russia
Will no more offer great art,
Will write great poetry

Which will harass the conscience
Of the earth *(TC: 53)*

Robin laments the sad condition of Myanmar, when he says "democracy weeping in its tropical forests" *(TC: 72)* and calls it a "mad country" *(TC:72)* and prefers the prevalence of Socialism for better development of the South Asian Countries exposing his support to the "Look East policy."

Temsula Ao, Monalisa Changkija and Robin S. Ngangom are three very important poets from the North-East India, who have landmark contributions to Indian English poetry. They have revealed some rare concepts in their socialist and feminist outlook and quests, which have not been achieved by their counterparts in the mainstream of Indian English writing. These poets write, so that poetry should move the heart of man and these inspirations should shepherd him into green pastures. The poets remind readers that, every individual has unlimited liberty in the state of nature, which can be channeled in constructive paths. This Socialism rises above individual interests, to the higher interests of the society as a whole. The themes and styles of the poets have earned them a foremost place in the North-East literature, and on the national and international front. The three writers do not agree with the Marxian perspective, that the predominance of man in marriage is simply a consequence of his economic predominance and will vanish with it automatically. But they agree with the Marxian view that true equality between the sexes, could only be achieved in a socialist society and that the sexual class system can only end, when women cease to be slaves to their biology. The collective unconscious, paves the way for a collective unconsciousness when it comes to the rights of women in the society. The derogatory stereotypes of women in literature mostly written by men are pitied upon by the three writers. Till recently, the women characters in literature were stereotypes, meant to manifest the shameless acceptance of the subjugation of the second sex by men. They had definite roles to play, chiefly as objects to gratify men's sexual urges.

The interior of the modern Indian social structure is scrutinized by these three eminent writers in their poems. They examine the role of women in society in relation to that of man, from a psychological perspective too. They are, three of the few poets who can write well on both politics and love and not be afraid of showing their links. Temsula Ao, Monalisa Changkija and Robin S. Ngangom are three very important poets from the North-East India, who have landmark contributions to Indian English poetry. They have revealed some rare concepts in their socialist and feminist outlook and quests, which have not been achieved by their counterparts in the mainstream of Indian English writing. These poets write, so that poetry should move the heart of man and these inspirations should shepherd him into green pastures. The poets remind readers that, every individual has unlimited liberty in the state of nature, which can be channeled in constructive paths. This Socialism rises above individual interests, to the higher interests of the society as a whole. The themes and styles of the poets have earned them a foremost place in the North-East literature, and on the national and international front.)

The poets take us on a journey, through the dark hearts of the North-East Indian society, where one finds innocent women weeping for their dead husbands, mothers shedding tears for their sons, for the young men often fall prey to the hands of the anti-social elements fighting for the wrong cause. Feminism for these born writers, differ from what actually is thought of as Feminism. It is not a cry in favor of the doctrine advocating social, political, and all other rights of women equal to those of men. Feminism is about accepting women as they are. Many consider women as physically and emotionally weak; this is true only when they are compared to men. The poets ask a pertinent question at this juncture, why should men and women be compared at all, they are different biologically making it impossible for any sort of comparisons. Women are physically strong when they are not compared with men and emotionally they are matured, why should there be a comparison at all?

Temsula Ao and Monalisa Changkija are not mere romantic poets of the Second Sex, nor is Robin S. Ngangom male, writing poetry for its own sake. The former two are accomplished feminist philosophers also. Their philosophy of life is not written in prose but in verse. Perhaps the assumption that, there are no great woman philosophers would come to an end gradually as these writers get recognition from the male-dominated sphere of philosophers. They mirror the conditions and struggles of women in their society. Temsula Ao, Monalisa Changkija and perhaps, even Robin S. Ngangom echo the thoughts, and the words of Betty Williams, the Nobel Prize winner *(1979),*

> The voice of women has a special role and a special soul force in the struggle for a non violent world. *(Davies. 2006: 178)*

Poetry is used by them as a tool, to air their views upon diverse issues, such as Feminism and Socialism. For them Feminism is a philosophy in which women and their contributions are valid. They bridge many postmodern poetic movements.

The three poets have reaffirmed through their poems that, women and men are fundamentally the same, thus contradicting that humanity is male, and man defines woman not in herself, but as relative to him and not an autonomous being. The truth of Socialism and Feminism that are entwined on the foot-hills of the poetical works of Temsula Ao, Monalisa Changkija and Robin S. Ngangom, is examined as to how far it could cater, to the good of man and society, because poetry is the one great agency, in the regeneration of mankind. The poets have an enthusiasm for humanity and so believed, in the dawning of a new day, just as Shelley,

> Mankind appear to me to be emerging from their trance. I am aware; methinks, of a slow, gradual, silent change." *(Buchan.1990: 435.)*

The 21st century, known as the age of interrogation and anxiety, make a significant departure from the past, challenging authority, asserting rights and exposing the hollowness of the way of the world. It is an age of self-consciousness where writers are intensely critical of the composition of society. Temsula Ao, Monalisa Changkija, and Robin S. Ngangom joyfully greet the self- consciousness revolution. Their poems prove so, sympathizing with the underdog, scorning shams and affectations. Reading their poetry, one understands that we are only beginning to know what each one is capable of. They poetize of a new world built on justice and love. These poets impress upon humanity, that for a moment, it seemed as if leaving behind the evils of the past, humanity at large was to pass forward immediately into an era of realized democratic ideals - of liberty, brotherhood and the rights of man. The three poets have further powered their poems on feministic values, believing that a woman's physical difference enables her to experience, feel, and think differently. Hence, what women write is what they ought to write. The poets have enriched Feminism with their revolutionary and innovative ideas.

Temsula Ao, Monalisa Changkija and Robin S. Ngangom rise above contemporary poets of North-East India, for their flavored poems, with wonderful humanitarian enthusiasm and gorgeous dreams of progress. In a flash of perception one understands that, they are poets who are beacons of hope for humanity. Their sense for mankind is not buried but brews rays of progressive promises. These poets have waved the wand of poetry, to an excellent advantage to nudge man to a right direction, re-shaping human thoughts, lives and relationships, refining and polishing each individual. The poetry of Temsula Ao, Monalisa Changkija and Robin S. Ngangom, are a personification of a 'Kingmaker' endeavouring to, Paradise Regained, perhaps?

Bibliography

(A) PRIMARY SOURCES

(i) Books

Ao, Temsula

_______________*1988. Songs That Tell.* Calcutta: Writers Workshop.

_______________*1992. Songs That Try to Say.* Calcutta: Writers Workshop.

_______________*1995. Songs of Many Moods.* New Delhi: Har-Anand Publications.

_______________*2003. Songs from Here and There.* Shillong: NEHU Publications.

_______________*2006. These Hills called Home.* New Delhi: Penguin.

_______________*2007. Songs From The Other Life.* Pune: Grasswork Books.

Changkija, Monalisa

_______________*1993. Weapons of Words on Pages of Pain.* Dimapur: Write-on Publications.

_______________*2007. Monsoon Mourning.* Dimapur: Write-on Publications.

Ngangom, Robin S.

_______________*1988. Words and the Silence.* Calcutta: Writers Workshop.

_______________*1994. Time's Crossroads.* Hyderabad: Disha Books, Orient Longman Ltd.

——————*2006. The Desire of Roots.* Cuttack: Chandrabhaga Publications.

——————*1993. Anthropology of New Indian English Poetry.* (ed). Makarand Paranjape New Delhi: Rupa & Co.

——————*1995. Khasia in Gwalia.* Wales: Alun Books.

——————*2000. A New Book of Indian Poems in English.* Calcutta: Writers Workshop.

——————*2005. Confronting Love: Poems,* New Delhi: Penguin Books Pvt Ltd.

(ii) Papers/Articles/Reviews/Interviews

Temsula Ao

——————*2006. These Hills Called Home: Stories From A War Zone.* http://www.tribuneindia.com/2006/20060326/spectrum/book10.htm

——————*2007*. Interview by Rosaline Jamir. 13th Oct. Inspirations: *Songs That Tell & Songs of Many Moods.* Shillong.

——————*2008*. Interview by Ashley Tellis. *The Agony of Rebirth.* Chennai. Indian Express: Sunday Section-II. I Witness.

——————*2008*. Interview by Rosaline Jamir. 24th April. Impressions: *Songs from Here and There.* Dimapur.

——————*2008*. Interview by Rosaline Jamir. 5th June & 10th Oct. Believing In: *Songs That Try to Say.* Shillong.

——————*2008.* Yajangla's Story Or Supernatural Transformation. 15th Nov. Tribal World of North-East India. ISHANI - Vol. 11. No.6. 1.

——————*2009. India'09- Through Fresh Eyes-Literature of conflict*. 21st April. http://www.londonbookfair.co.uk/page.cfm/Action=Seminars/SeminarID=25

Monalisa Changkija

——————*1992. "Not be Dead."* 23rd Sept. After the assassination of Charlie Kevichusa. *URA MAIL* Editor. Dimapur: *URA MAIL.*

——————*2004. Poetry and the Northeast :Foraging for a destiny.* 7th Nov. http://www.hindu.com/lr/2004/11/07/stories/2004110700350500.htm

——————*2005. Contributions of the Vernacular and Small Newspapers Towards Development.* 9th Aug. On invitation to the Kamala Saikia Memorial Trust. Guwahati. http://kamalasaikia.com/article3.html

——————*2006.* Interview by Rosaline Jamir. 20th Oct. Penning Pain: *Weapons of Words on Pages of Pain.* Dimapur.

——————*2007. Light the Lamp of Democracy.* 29th Sept. Special Contribution. The Seoul Times. http://theseoultimes.com/ST/?url=/ST/db/read.php?idx=5699

——————*2007.* Book review speech: *Monsoon Mourning* by Joyti George Roy. 17th Sept. Dimapur: Saramati Hotel.

——————*2007.* Poetry Recitation. *Monsoon Mourning* by Rosaline Jamir. 17th Sept. Dimapur: Saramati Hotel.

——————*2007. Nagas call for tougher action against Junta.* 6th Oct. http://www.citizen-news.org/2007/10/nagas-call-for-tougher-action-against.html?showComment=1191793080000

——————*2008.* Interview by Rosaline Jamir. 17th Oct. Memorabilia: *Monsoon Mourning.* Dimapur.

Robin S. Ngangom

——————*1995.* "Poems". *Indian Literature*; 168, July-Aug. New Delhi: Sahitya Akademi. (125-128).

——————*1999.* "Three Poems". *Indian Literature.* 190. Mar- April. New Delhi: Sahitya Akademi. (54-56).

———————*2000*. "Robin S. Ngangom: A Poet of the Soil" in New Quest, (An Interdisciplinary Journal of Society and Culture), http://www.loyolacollege.edu/profile/english/Prof.T.R.Joy.pdf

———————*2000*.(a). " Three Poems". *Indian Literature*. 197. May- June. New Delhi; Sahitya Akademi. (37-40).

———————*2000*.(b). " Four Poems" *Chandrabhaga*. Vol.2. Cuttak: Chandrabhaga Society, (25-31).

———————*2002*. " Seven Poems" *Indian Literature*. (Sept.- Oct.) New Delhi. Sathiya Academi.. (93-101).

———————*2003*. " Seven Poems" *Chandrabhaga*. Vol.8. Cuttak: Chandrabhaga Society.(27-28).

———————*2006*. *Poetry in a Time of Terror*. http://www.sarai.net/publications/readers/06-turbulence/03_robin.pdf

———————*2006*. In Conversation: Robin S. Ngangom and Guru Ladakhi. March – April. *Catscanned*, No. 2. Gangtok.

———————*2007*. Interview by Rosaline Jamir. 6th Oct & 12th Dec. Of. *Time's Crossroads* & *Words and the Silence*. Shillong.

———————*2009*. Interview by Rosaline Jamir. 5th March & 12th May. Wishful Thinking? *The Desire of Roots*. Shillong.

(B). SECONDARY SOURCES

Abrams, M.H . *1997*. *A Glossary of Literary Terms*. Bangalore: A Prism Indian Edition.

——————— *1993*. *A Glossary of Literary Terms*. Madras: Macmillian (Rpt.)

Adiga, Aravind. *2008*. *White Tiger*. New Delhi: Harper Collins Publishers.

Agarwal, Bina.*1997*. "The Gender and Environment Debate: Lessons from India." *The Women Development and*

Gender Reader. (ed). N. Visvanathan. London: Zed Books.

Avineri, Shlomo. *1968. The Social and Political Thought of Karl Marx.* New Delhi: S.Chand & Company Ltd, Cambridge Univ Press.

Bai, K. Meera. *1996.* " The Literary Backdrop": *Women's Voice : The Novels of Indian Women Writers:* New Delhi: Prestige. pp.9-15.

Bakka, Olive. *1981. Faces of Feminism as a Social Movement.* New York: St. Martin's Press.

Baral, K.C. *2007.* " Indian Writing in English: Mapping the Terrain": *Contemporary Indian Writing in English.* Ed.N.Das. New Delhi : Adhyayan Publishers, pp. 1-9.

Barua, Indira. et al. *2002., Ethnic Groups Cultural Continuities and Social Changes in North East India.* New Delhi: Mittal Publications.

Barry, Peter. *1995 (1999). Beginning Theory: An Introduction to Literary and Cultural Theory.* Manchester & New York: Manchester University Press.

Baruah, Sanjib. *2005. Durable Disorder:* Understanding the Politics of North East India. New Delhi: OUP.

Baveja, J. D. *1982. New Horizons of North East.* Guwahati: Western Book Depot.

Behera, M. C. *2000. Tribal Religion: Change and Continuity.* New Delhi: Commonwealth Publishers.

Bertens, Hans. *2001 (2004). Literary Theory: The Basics.* London and New York: Routledge.

Beteille, Andre. *1974. Social Inequality.* New Delhi: Oxford University Press.

Bhardwaj, Ashwani. *2006. Speeches by Great Personalities.* New Delhi: Goodwill Publishing House.

Bhatnagar, Manmohan K. *1998.* "Indian English Literature: Its Rationale and a Critical Introduction" *Indian*

Writings in English. New Delhi: Atlantic Publishers and Distributors.

———————— *2002.* "Feminist English Literature. An Introduction": *Feminist English,* (ed) M.K. Bhatnagar: New Delhi: Atlantic, pp.1-3.

Bhattacharjee, K.K. *1983. North East India: A Study.* New Delhi: Cosmo Publications.

Bhelande, Anjali et al.(ed) *2000. Articulating Gender.* New Delhi: Pencraft International.

Bose, N.K. *1967. Culture and Society in India.* Bombay: Asia Publishing House.

Buchan, John (ed). *1990. A History of English Literature.* New Delhi: Anmol Publications.

Cavallaro, Dani. *2001. Critical and Cultural Theory.* London: The Athlone Press.

Cazamian & Legouis. *1996. History of English Literature.* New Delhi: Macmillan Indian Limited.

Cervantes de Miguel.*1605-1615. Don Quixote.* New York City: W.W. Norton & Company.

Chandra , N.D.R. *2004. Modern Indian Writing in English: Critical Perception Vol-1.* New Delhi: Sarup & Sons.

Chandra, N.D.R. & Nigamananda Das. *2007. Ecology, Myth and Mystery: Contemporary Poetry in English from North East India.* New Delhi: Sarup & Sons.

Channa, S. (ed). *2004. Encyclopedia of Feminist Theory Vol – I.* New Delhi: Cosmo Publications.

———————— (ed). *2004. Encyclopedia of Feminist Methodology Vol – II.* New Delhi: Cosmo Publications.

———————— (ed). *2004. Encyclopedia of Feminism and literature Vol – III.* New Delhi: Cosmo Publications.

Chatterji, Shoma A.*1989. The Indian Women's Search for An Identity.* New Delhi: Vikas Publishing House Pvt. Ltd.

Chopra, J.K. *2007. Unique Quintessence of Society of India.* (Rev.) New Delhi: Unique Publishers.

Choudhury, Bibhash. *2005. Nagaland University: Anthology of Poetry (ed).* Kolkota: Macmillan India Limited.

Collier, Peter. et al. (eds). *1997. Literary Theory Today.* New York: Cornell University Press.

————————— *2002. Twentieth Century Literary Criticism.* New Delhi: Atlantic Publishers.

Cuddon, J.A. *(1977). Dictionary of Literary Terms & Literary Theory.* Penguin Books Ltd.

Das, Kamala. *1985.* "An Introduction" : *Indian English Poetry since 1950: An Anthology.* ed Vilas Sarang. Bombay: Orient Longman, pp.76,77.

Das, Lakshahira. *1990. Between Births.* Guwahati: Sangam.

Das, Nigamananda *.2004. Mosaic of Redemption: Essays on Poetry in English from North East.* Cuttack: M.G.Publications.

————————— *2009*(b). "Multi-Ethnic Poetry in English from North East India: Thematic Trends and Concepts." Multicultural Literature in India: *Critical Perceptions. ed.* N.D.R. Chandra. New Delhi: Sarup & Sons. 01-26.

Das, Veena Noble. *1995.* "Feminism and Literature". *Feminism and Literature.* ed. Veena Noble Dass. New Delhi: Prestige pp. 9-12.

Davidawson,Christel.*2000.* "Feminist theories". *Literary Criticism and Theory: Block 6.* New Delhi: IGNOU.pp.7-47.

Davidow, Ellen Messer. *1994.* "Feminist Theory and Criticism: 1963-1972". *The John Hopkins Guide to Literary Theory and Criticism.* Michael Groden and Martin Kreiswirth.(eds.) London : The John Hopkins University Press.pp.231-236.

Davies, Smith. *2006. Women Who Changed the World.*

Fifty inspirational women who shaped history. London: Smith-Davis Publishing Ltd.

De Beauviour, Simone. *1953 (1997). The Second Sex.* London : Vintage.

Debi, Renu. *1987. Progress of Education in Assam.* Guwahati: Western Book Depot.

Deka, Phani. *2007. The Great Indian Corridor in the East.* New Delhi: Mittal Publications.

Delmar Rosalind. *1986.* "What is Feminism?" *What is Feminism?* Juliet Mitchell and Ann Oakley. (eds) New York: Pantheon Books.

Desai, Kiran. *2006. Inheritance of Loss.* Paperback. New Delhi: Penguin Books.

Dubey, Leela (ed). *1996. Caste: It's Twentieth Century Avtar.* New Delhi: Viking Penguin India.

——————— *1997. Women and Kinship: Comparative Perspectives on Gender in South and South East Asia.* New Delhi: Sage Publications.

Dubey, S.C. *1990. Society of India.* New Delhi: National Book Trust.

Dubey, S M.*1978. North East India: A Sociological study.* Delhi: Concept Publishing Company.

Dussel, Enrique. *1985. Philosophy of Liberation.* Maryknoll, New York: Orbis Books.

Dyer, Wayne. W. *1997. Manifest Your Destiny.* Harper Collins.

Eagleton, Mary. *1986.* (ed) "Gender and Genre". *Feminist Literary Theory: A Reader.* UK: Basil Blackwell Ltd.pp.88-92.

——————— *1994. Feminist Literary Theory.* Cambridge: Blackwell.

Essel, Philomeno, et al. (ed). *2005. A Companion to Gender Studies.* Jaipur: Rawat Publications with Blackwell.

Everden, Neil. *1992. The Social Creation of Nature.* Baltimore.

Edacheriparambil, Tomy. *1990. Gitanjali.* Bangalore: Claretian Publications.

Foucault, M. *1973. Madness and Civilization: A History of Insanity in the Age of Reason.* (1st ed 1965). New York: Vintage Books.

Freud, Sigmund. *1993.* "On Dreams" *Art in Theory: 1900-1990.* Charles Harrison and Paul Wood (eds) Cambridge: Blackwell Publishing Inc.pp.26-34.

Friedan Betty.*1963. The Feminine Mystique.* New York City : W. W. Norton & Company.

Geismare, Maxwell. *1942. Writers in Crisis.* Boston: Houghton Hifflin.

Ghurye, G.S. *1980. The Burning Cauldron of North-East India.* Bombay:Popular Prakashan Private Ltd.

Goodman, W.R. *2004. Contemporary Literary Theory.* Delhi: Doaba Publications.

Gopalakrishnan, R. *1991. The North-East India Land, Economy and People.* New Delhi: Vikas Publishing House Pvt Ltd.

Green,Gayle & Coppelia Kahn. (eds). *1985. Making a Difference Feminist Literary Criticism.* London: Metheun.

Greene, Robert. *1999. The 48 Laws of Power.* London: Viva Books Pvt. Ltd. p. 191.

Guerin, Wilfred L. et al. *2005. A Handbook of Critical Approaches to Literature.* New York: OUP.

Guha, Ananya Sankar. *2000.* "Poetry and the English Writing Scene"*: Trends in Social Sciences and Humanities in North East India.* Shillong. pp. 117-125.

Haralambos, Michael.et al. *1980. Sociology Themes and Perspectives.* New Delhi: Oxford University Press.

Hawthorne, Nathaniel. *1851 (1981). The House of the Seven Gables: A Romance.* New York: Bantam Classic.

Hutchinson, Thomas (ed). *1970. Shelley Poetical Works.* New York: Oxford University Press.

Iyengar. K.R.S. *1943. Literature and Authorship in India.* London: Allen & Unvrin.

———————— *1946. The Indian Contribution to English Literature.* Bombay: Karnatak Publishing House.

———————— *1973. Indian Writings in English.* Bombay: Asia Publising House.

———————— *1990. Indian Writing in English.* New Delhi: Sterling Pvt Ltd.

Keller, Catherine . *1990.* " Women Against the Wasting the World : Notes and Eschatology and Ecology," *Reviewing the world : The Emergence of Ecofeminism.* ed. I. Diamond & G.F. Orenstein. San Francisco : Sierra Club Books.

King, Bruce. *1987. Modern Indian Poetry in English.* New Delhi: Oxford University Press.

King, Bruce. *1998. New National and Post-colonial Literatures: An Introduction.* Oxford: Clavendon Paperbacks.

Kumar, Gajendra and Uday Ojha. *2005. Indian English Literature. A Postcolonial Response.* New Delhi: Sarup & Sons.

Kumar, Satish. *2005. Contemporary Criticism and Theory.* Agra: Laxmi Narain Aggarwal.p. 9.

Kunjakkan, K. A. *2002. Feminism and Indian Realities.* New Delhi: Mittal Publications.

Kynpham, Singh & Ngangom, Robin S. *2003. Anthology of Contemporary Poetry From the Northeast.* Shillong: NEHU Publications.

Lenin, Vladimir I. *1934. On the Emancipation of Women.* New York International.

Long, William J. *1989. English Literature: Its History and Its Significance.* New Delhi: Kalyani Publishers.

Loomba, Ania. *1998. Colonialism / Post-colonialism.* London and New York: Routledge.

Mahajan, V.D. *1998. Political Theory.* New Delhi: S. Chand & Company Ltd.

Malpas, Simon et al. *2006. The Routledge Companion to Critical Theory.* London and New York: Routledge.

Martin, Francis. *1994. The Feminist Question Feminist Theology in the Light of Christian Tradition.* Edinburgh: T&T Clark Ltd.

Megu, Kangki. *2007. Development Issues in North-East Region.* New Delhi: Mittal Publications.

Miller, D. *1976. Social Justice.* New York: Oxford University Press.

Miller, David. *2005. Political Philosophy: A Very Short Introduction.* New York: Oxford University Press.

Minogue, Sally. *1990.* (ed) "Introduction: Problems for Feminist Criticism" *Problems for Feminist Criticism.* London: Routledge.pp.1-4.

Mishra, D.S. *2004.* "Modern Indian Writing in English: An Overview". *Modern Indian Writing in English: Critical Perspectives.* Vol.1. N.D.R.Chandra. (ed.) New Delhi: Sarup and Sons.pp.1-47.

Mohanty, Satya P.*1998. "Identity, Multiculturalism Justice". Literary Theory and the Claims of* History, Post Modernism, Objectivism, Multicultural Politics. New Delhi: *OUP, pp.198-253.*

Momsen, J. *1995. Women and Development in the Third World.* London: Routledge. Nayar, Pramod K. *2002. Literary Theory Today.* New Delhi: Prestige.

Nelson, Thomas. *1987. The Holy Bible.* Nashville: Thomas Nelson Publishers. Newman, Michael. *2005.*

Socialism: A Very Short Introduction. New York: Oxford University Press.

Nicholson, Linda (ed). *1997. The Second Wave: A Reader in Feminist Theory.* New York: Routledge.

Nongkynrih, K.S. *2007. Around The Hearth: Khasi Legends.* New Delhi: Penguin.

Oliver, Kelly. *1995. Womanizing Nietzsche: Philosophy Relation to the "Feminine."* New York: Routledge.

Orwell, George. *2005. Animal Farm.* Delhi: Surjeet Publications.

Palkar Sarla. *1996.* "Feminst Literary Theory: Creating New Maps": *Indian Response to Literary Theories* (ed). R.S. Pathak. New Delhi : Creative Books, pp. 185-197.

Panja, Shormistha. (ed) *2002. Critical Theory: Textual Application.* New Delhi: World View.

Parasher, S.V. *1996.* "Code-switching / code-mixing:" *Introduction To Linguistics.* Block.V. Hyderabad: CIEFL, p.18.

Pope, Rob. *2001. The British Studies Book: An Introduction to Language, Literature and Culture.* London : Routledge.

Prakash, Anand. (ed). *2002. Marxism.* New Delhi: Worldview.

Pruthi, Raj. et al. *1995. Women Education and Culture.* New Delhi: Anmol Publications Pvt Ltd.

Quinn, Edward. *2000. A Dictionary of Literary and Thematic Terms.* New York: Checkmark Books.

Ramaswami, Sushila. *2003. Political Theory.* Madras: Macmilian India Ltd.

Rege, Sharmila. *2003. Sociology of Gender: The Challenge of Feminist Sociological Knowledge.* New Delhi: Sage Publications India Pvt. Ltd.

Rendulich, Joseph. S. *2004. Spirit and Matter.* New Delhi: Phoenix International Publishers.

Ricket, Arthur Compton. *2004. A History of English Literature.* New Delhi: UBS Publishers Distributors Pvt. Ltd.

Ritzer, George. *1986. Indian Sociology: Social Conditioning and Emerging Trends.* New Delhi: Vist.

Robin, Louis (ed). *1982. A Tragedy of Two Lost Women: America Literature in Context.* London: Hethuen.

Rowbotham, Sheila. *1972. Women Renaissance and Revolution.* Penguin.

———— *1992. Women in Movement: Feminism and Social Action.* New York: Routledge.

Roy, Arundhati. *1997. The God of Small Things.* New Delhi: IndiaInk.

Sabastian, A.J. et al. *2005. Poetry from Nagaland.* New Delhi: Savio P. Pvt. Ltd.

Sarang, Vilas. *1989* (1995) (ed) *Indian English Poetry since 1950: An Anthology*, Bombay: Orient Longman.

Sarin, VIK. *1980. India's North–East in Flames.* New Delhi: Vikas Publishing House Pvt Ltd.

Satish, Kumar. *2007. Indo-Anglian Poetry.* Agra: The Publishers.

Saunders, Kriemild (ed). *2004. Feminist Post- Development Thought.* New Delhi: Zubaan.

Scholes, Robert. et al. (4th ed). *2004. Elements of Literature.* New York: Oxford University Press.

Scott, James. *1946.* The Making of Literature. UK: Secker and Warburg.p.48.

Sen, Geeti. *2006. Where the Sun Rises When Shadows Fall The North – East.* New Delhi: Oxford University Press.

Shankar Rao, C.N. (rev).*2006. Principal of Sociology with*

an Introduction to Social Thought New Delhi: S. Chand & Company Ltd.

Shiva Vandana 1988. *Staying Alive: Women, Ecology and Development*. London: Zed Books.

Sharma, Abhishek. *2001. Changing Modern Society.* New Delhi: Mittal Publications.

Sharma, Y.K. *2007. Indian Society: Issues and Problems.* Agra: Lakshmi Narain Agarwal.

Showalter, Elaine. *1977. Women Writing and Writing about Women.* London: Croom Helm.

Sinha, K.K.. *2000.* "Stemming the Rot: The Rising Women with Promising Vistas Ahead". *Indian Writings in English, Vol.IX* . Manmohan K. Bhatnagar and M. Rajeshwar.(eds)New Delhi: Atlantic Publishers and Distributers.p.211.

Spivak, G. *1988. In Other Worlds: Essays in Cultural Politics*. New York & London: Routledge.

Srinivas, M.N. *1980. Social Structure.* New Delhi: Hindustan Publishing House.

Srinivas, M.N. *1963. Social Changes in India.* California, Berkeley: University of California Press.

Sturgeon, N. *1997. Ecofeminist Natures: Race, Gender, Feminist Theory and Political Action.* New York: Routledge.

Syiem, Almond D. *2003. "Poems": Anthology of Contemporary Poetry from the Northeast.* Shillong: North Eastern Hill University: pp 170-175.

Syiem, Esther. *2003. "Poems": Anthology of Contemporary Poetry from the Northeast.* Shillong: North Eastern Hill University: pp. 176-181.

——————— *2005. Oral Scriptings.* Calcutta: Writers Workshop.

Tagore, Rabindranath. *1913* (1966). *Gitanjali.* Madras: Macmillan. India Ltd.

Tagore, Rabindranath. *1996. Gitanjali: Song offerings.* Mumbai: Reprint Macmillan India Ltd.

Tewari, R P. *1989. Development and problems of Education in N.E. India.* Shillong: Akashi Book Depot.

Tana, Yumlam. *2003. "Poems": Anthology of Contemporary Poetry from the Northeast.* NEHU. pp. 13-16.

Tharu, Susie. et al (eds). *1993. Women Writing in India.* New York: Feminist Press.

Warjri, Indari Syiem. *2003. "Poems": Anthology of Contemporary Poetry from the Northeast.* Shillong: North Eastern Hill University. pp. 188-192.

Walters, Margaret. *2005. Feminism: A Very Short Introduction.* New York: Oxford University Press.

Wattal, Ameeta Mulla. *1995*. "Feminism in Commonwealth Literature: A difference of View": *Feminism and Literature.* ed. Veena Noble Dass. New Delhi: Prestige, pp.13-20.

Weedon, Chris. *1987 (1995). Feminist Practice and Poststructuralist Theory.* Blackwell: Cambridge M A & Oxford UK.

Wilkinson, Sue & Kitzinger, Celia (ed).*1995. Feminism and Discourse: Psychological Perspectives.* New Delhi: Sage Publications.

Wisker, Gina. *2000.* "Writing by Women from the Indian Subcontinent". In Gina Wisker. *Postcolonial and African American Women's Writing: A Critical Introduction.* Hound Mills. I. London: Macmillan. Chap.8.pp. 179-201.

Woolf,Virginia.*1929. A Room of One's Own.* New Delhi: Ubs Publishers Distributors Ltd.

Wyatt, H.G. *1925. Stories From Shakespeare.* New York: Oxford University Press.

Yates, Gayle Graham. *1975. What Women Want: The Ideas of the Movement.*USA: Havard University Press.

Zeitlin, Irving M (Rep). *2004. Rethinking Sociology: A Critique of Contemporary Theory* Jaipur: Rawat Publications.

Zote, Mona. *2003. "Poems": Anthology of Contemporary Poetry from the Northeast.* Shillong: North Eastern Hill University: pp. 199-205.

Research Papers and Articles (Journals/Magazines)

Allen, Richard. *1998.* "Literature, Gender, Feminist Criticism." *A Handbook to Literary Research.* Simon Eliot and W.R. Owens. (eds.) London: Routledge.pp.117-130.

Anjum, Hasan. *1995.* "Women on Pages of Pain." Guwahati: *The Assam Tribune. May 14th.*

Chanana, Kuhu. *2005.* "An Exploration of the Repressive Module of Sexuality in Modern Indian Women Writers: Namita Gokhale, Krishna Sobti and Ismat Chuti," *Indian Literature.* 49.6 Nov- Dec.pp.162-176.

Chatterjee, Paramita. *2006.* "The Fantasists" *India Today.* November 20th. p. 80

Das, Bijay Kumar. *1999.* " The Language of *The God of Small Things :* A Post- colonial Study". *The Journal of Indian Writing in English.* Vol.27, pp.36-38.

Das, Nigamananda. *1998(b)."The Poetry of Robin S. Ngangom": Dialogue III. Ed. N. Nagaraju.*Doimukh: NEIFES. 94-99.

———————— *2000(a). "The Poets of Nagaland Writing in English": Dialogue -IV&V. (ed). N.D.R. Chandra.* Kohima: NEIFES. 140-153.

———————— *2003.* "Nostalgic Matrices: Poetry in English from Meghalaya". JFES. 21-32.

———————— *2003(a). Vision Vigorous. Souvenir of ICPR sponsored National Seminar on* Feminism & Self Expression. North Lakhimpur: Lakhimpur Girls'College. p.17.

——————— *2008. "The Poetry of Monalisa Changkija: An Ecofeminist Reading." Rock Pebbles International Literary Magazine.* Jaipur: Rock Pebbles *Vol. XII.* No. 11 Publication. p.*1.*

Jamir, Rosaline. *2005. Poetry from Nagaland: A Review.* Dimapur: *Eastern Mirror, 21st Nov. p.5.*

Karat, Prakash. *2005.* "People's Democracy": *Weekly Organ of the Communist Party of India.* (Marxist). Vol. XXIX.No.52 Dec. 25, pp. 1,2.

Loomis, roger Sherman. *1919.* " A Defence of Naturalism". *International Journal of Ethics.* Vol.29 Jan. 1919.pp. 188-201.

Mahanta, Amrit Joyti. *2006.* "A Different landscape." *Literary Review.* The Hindu. Online Edition. 7th May.

Mannen, T N. *2008. 33% Reservation for Women:* Dimapur: *Eastern Mirror, 25th Sept. p.7.*

Margolis, Diane Rothbard. *1993.* " Women's Movement around the World: Cross Cultural Comparisons" *Gender and Society,* Vol.7. No.3. Sept. pp.379-399.

Mukherjee, Pranab. *2009. "Status of Women":* Dimapur: Nagaland Post. 25th Feb. *p.1.*

Murphy, Patrick. D. *2009.*"Women Writers: Spiritual Realism, , Ecological Responsibility and Inhabitation." *Journal of Literature, Culture and Media Studies Contemporary Women Writings.* Chhattisgarh: Chandra Publications. pp. 5-11.

Phukan, Mitra. *1998. New Frontiers.* A Journal of the North-East. Guwahati: Writer's Forum. Vol. 1:1.

Rajan P.K.*2006.* "Indian English Literature: Changing Traditions." *LitCritt.* Issue 61 and 62. June & Dec. Vol.32. No. 1&2.pp.11-23.

Sen, Soumen et al. *1987.* "Folk Songs of the North Eastern Hills": *Indian Literature:* 120 (July-Aug) (ed) S. Balu Rao. New Delhi: Sahitya Akademi. pp 11-34.

Sharma, Anjana. *1998.* "Rescuing the Past" *Outlook*. March 23.p.108.

Singh, B. N. *2000.* "Lamenting the Destruction of Harsh and Lovely Land: Feminists Response to Ecology": *Dialogue IV & V.* ed. N.D.R. Chandra. Kohima: NEIFES. pp.1-8.

Solzhenitsyn, Alexander. *1967. "Open Letter to the Forth Soviet Writers Congress" 16th. May.*

Subramaniam, Mangala. *2004.* "The Indian Women's Movements", *Contemporary Sociology*. Vol.33. No.6. Nov.2004. pp. 635-639.

Swain, Rabindra K. *2004.* "Some Things are Sacred, an essay". *Chandrabhaga*. Vol.9. Cuttack: Chandrabhaga Society. pp. 115-127.

Velayudhan, Meera. *1994.* "Changing Roles and Women's Narratives" *Social Scientist*. Vol. 2, No.1/2 (Jan-Feb.). pp.64-79.

WEBSITES

(a) < www.raimes.com/camus2.htm >.

(b) < www.poetryfoundation.org/archive/poem.html?id=179569 >.

(c) < www. womenswriting.com>.

(d) < www.india.poetryinternationalweb.org >.

(e) < www.poemhunter.com/poem/bogland>.

(f) < www.internal.org/view_poem.phtml?poemID=356>.

(g) < www.ecofem.org/journal.htnl >.

(h) < www.loyolacollege.edu/profile/english/Prof.T.R.Joy.pdf>.

(i) < www.encyclopedia.com/doc/1G2-3404705322.html. >.

(j) <www.hinduism.about.com/cs/art/a/aa020904a.htm>

(k) <www.altavista.com>

(l) <www.hotbot.com>

(m) <www.google.com>

(n) <www.bing.com>

(o) 'Beowulf' <www.alcyone.com/max/lit/beowulf/>

(p) Feminism – Wikipedia :< www.wikipedia.org/wiki/ feminism>.

(q) Frossad, David. <www.postcolonial/web.org/india/ literature/maitil.html>.

(r) Felluga, Dino. *2003*. "Modules on Lacan: On Psychosexual Development. Introductory Guide to Critical Theory. <www.purdue.edu/guidetotheory/ psychoanalysis/lacandevelop. html>pp.1-10.

(s) Leachy, Terry. *1998*. "Ecofeminism as Practised: Gender and Environment in Culture and Politics Today" < www.octapod.org.8000/gifteconomy/context/ zcdgend-two.html>.

(t) Lye, John. *1996*. Psychoanalysis and Literature". *The Journal of Social and Psychological Sciences.* <www.geocities.com/Athens/Academy/4573/Lectures/ Feminism.html>pp.1-5

(u) Lye, John. *1997 (1998)*. "Some Issues in Postcolonial Theory". <www.brocku.ca/english/courses/4F70/ Postcol.html>

(v) ——— *1997 (1998)*. "Postcolonial Literature". Problems with the Term. <www.brocku.ca/english/ courses/4F70/Postcol.html>

(w) Macaulay, Thomas. *1835*. "Macaulay's Minute on Indian Education." 2nd Feb. <www.indianofficer.com/ forums/history-wiki/1997-macaulays-minute-indian-education.html>

(x) Manian, H.K. Ecofeminism Within Gender and Development". < www.ecofem.org/journal.html>.

(y) Plumwood, Val. "Nature, Self and Gender: Feminism, Environmental Philosophy and the critique of

Rationalism" <www2.feiffer.edu/~tridener/courses/ecowarm.html>.

(z) Rajan, Rajeshwari Sunder.*2001*. "Writing in English in India, Again."pp.1-5. <www.hinduonnet.com/2001/02/18/stories /1318067m.htm>

(aa) Salleh, Ariel kay. *1998*. "Epistemology and Metaphors of production: An Ecofeminist Reading of Critical Theory." *Studeis in the Hunanities.*(ed). Patrick Murphy, special issue of Feminism, Ecology and the Future of the Humanities 15.2. pp.130-139. <www.2.feiffer.edu/-tridener/courses/ecowarm. html>

(ab) Sunderajan, Rajeshwari.*2001*. "Writing in English in India, Again." Sunday, 18th Feb.pp.1-5. <www.hinduonnet.com/2001/02/18/stories / 1318067m.htm>

(ac) Tajero, Antonio Navarro. "Modern Indian Women Writers in English." *Literature in English Post-1914*. Ian MacKean(ed.). London: Hodder Arnold.pp.1-6. <www.literature_ study_online. com/essays/indian-women-book.html>

(ad) Thiruganananam, Jayalakshmi.*2008*. "The Status of Women Writers in India." <www.chillibreeze.co/articles/womenwritersinindiaandthepoweroftheirwriting.>p.1

(ae) Twine, R. J . "Ecofeminsim in Process." < www.ecofem.org/journal.html>.

(af) Warren, Karen. "Introduction to Ecofeminism" : Environmental Philosophy: From Animal Rights to Radical Ecology. <www2.feiffer.edu/~tridener/courses/ecowarm.html>

LIBRARIES CONSULTED

1. Eastern Christian College, Padumpukhuri, Dimapur: Nagaland.
2. Nagaland University Central Library, Kohima: Nagaland.

3. (a) North Eastern Hill University, Shillong, Meghalaya.
   (b) State Library, Shillong, Meghalaya.
   (c) CIEFL, Shillong, Meghalaya.
4. Patkai Christian College Library, Chumukedima, Dimapur: Nagaland.
5. Salesian College Library, Nagarjan, Dimapur: Nagaland.
6. St. Xavier's College Library, Ahmedabad: Gujarat.

Thematic Impressions, and Inspirations of North-East India

NAGALAND "LAND OF FESTIVALS"

Dzukou Valley, Nagaland

"Nagaland's Hub–Dimapur"

Landscapes of Mizoram

"The Nightingale of the East"

Barapani Lake – SHILLONG: MEGHALAYA

Also called the "Scotland of the East"
Poets have sung, of the ecology of this land.

Arunachal Pradesh means "The land of the rising sun," is also known as"The Dawn lit Mountains".

Romancing......Kanchenjunga National Park. Sikkim.

Imphal Valley

Manipur literally meaning "A Jewelled Land."

Assam Abounds in Traditions

Tripura: Traditions and landscapes

Index